THE
SECRET
LIFE OF
SUPERMOM

THE
SECRET
LIFE OF
SUPERMOM

The Tricks and Truths About Having It All

by Kathy Buckworth

To Celia —
to a soon-to-be
Supermom.

Kathy Buckworth

SOURCEBOOKS, INC.
NAPERVILLE, ILLINOIS

Published by Sourcebooks, Inc.
P.O. Box 4410, Naperville, Illinois 60567-4410
(630) 961-3900
Fax: (630) 961-2168
www.sourcebooks.com

Library of Congress Cataloging-in-Publication Data

Buckworth, Kathy.
  The secret life of supermom : the tricks and truths about having it
all /
Kathy Buckworth.
      p. cm.
  Includes bibliographical references.
  ISBN 1-4022-0388-8 (alk. paper)
 1. Working mothers. 2. Working mothers--Humor. 3. Parenting. I.
Title.

HQ759.48.B83 2005
306.874'3--dc22

2004029935

Printed and bound in Canada
WC   10 9 8 7 6 5 4 3 2 1

To Steve, who makes me Super,
and Victoria, Alexander, Bridget, and Nicholas,
who make me Mom.

CONTENTS

ACKNOWLEDGMENTS

My children and my sanity would not be intact without my amazing husband, Steve Webster, and his seemingly endless capacity to love, support, and humor me. (I can be crabby.) He lets me sleep in every weekend morning; he took me to the Oak Room in the Algonquin Hotel when I needed it most; and he accepts my freakish aversion to minivans.

To my beautiful children who inspire and infuriate me at a head-snapping pace. All of this is down to you.

I need to acknowledge my Encouragement Task Force: The Loyalty Chicks (Robynne Ostry, Leslie Rowland, Leslie McCauley, Ingrid Kasaks-Moyer, Ann McDermott, Susan Hum), The Baby Group Girls (Susan Michalek, Sue Valencia, Michelle Muscat, Marnie Escaf, Jackie Mann, Graydon Moffat), The Visa Babes (Cory Ellison, Deb Taras), and the assorted ears and shoulders of Eva Chan, Heather Hutchison, Sue Evans, Ally Collison, Michelle Mittermair, Sharon and Tony, "Big Dave" Flett, Susan and Des Webster, and the world's greatest babysitter, Margaret Buckworth. More wine for all.

Leslie Garrett deserves my thanks for giving me the first opportunity to say the words "I have a deadline."

Thanks to Deb Werksman, my editor, Supermom in her own right, for taking a chance on a sarcastic Canadian mind.

To Dorothy Parker, who inspired my own "fresh hell."

And to my nanny, who quit just before baby #4, and the vice president who convinced me that my lack of skill as a banker was exceeded only by a dearth of tact (and, by the way, everything is funny). I'm much better at this end of a Visa card.

P.S. Mum & Dad (a.k.a. John and Jill Buckworth)—thanks.

introduction:

"Show me a woman who doesn't feel guilt and I'll show you a man."

—Erica Jong

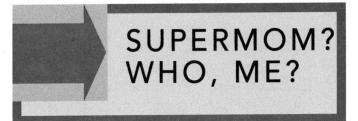

SUPERMOM?
WHO, ME?

Let me start by saying that I think I have it all. All I have to do now is to figure out how to give some of it back. Marriage, family, professional life. I've worked hard to get where I'm at, but it's simply too much sometimes. When the term Supermom first emerged, I thought it sounded wonderful. This was a fabulous woman who would swoop into the office, perform her professional duties while outfitted in a custom-made designer suit (maximum size 6). Then, tearing herself away from the accolades of her coworkers and superiors, due to her latest career triumph, she would breezily wind her way home (in a zippy little sports car, immaculate), and be greeted heartily at the front door by her charming and polished young family. No boring stay-at-home housewife à la Carol Brady for me. No, I was going to be this combination of Meg Ryan (for cuteness), Gloria Steinem (pre-marriage), and

Mother Earth (who bathed), all rolled into one fantastic fat-free package. Yeah, right.

What I didn't take into account was that every single minute of my "super" life would be totally consumed by the needs and wants of others. The balance between happy home life and successful career is similar to one of those plastic games one has as a child, where the object is to get each little silver ball in a cardboard hole at the same time. Just when you have one lined up, another one pops out to frustrate you. The day that you have to give the most important presentation of your career is the day at least three other things will go wrong. These things can include, but are not limited to: a child's illness ("drug 'em up and send 'em in" is a cry often heard from my parenting colleagues), nylons ripping open just as you get up from your desk to head to the boardroom, a forgotten note from school with the words PLEASE REMEMBER, MRS. BUCKWORTH! scrawled in the teacher's handwriting, a sprung piece of orthodontal wear, or simply a big, greasy pimple on your chin the day you run out of concealer.

You know you're in trouble when your child tells you she needs new sneakers for gym class and, after consulting your overflowing daytimer, you advise her that you would be happy to dash out and purchase these shoes for her...if she could just wait until a week from Tuesday. Reasonable, you think. She may point out that by that time she would have failed the physical education program due to "inadequate equipment." And you ask yourself how bad that would really be.

Earning the title of Supermom simply requires you to give up all personal time, self-identity, leisure activities, and patience. You too will be able to perform super tasks like taking conference calls at home while running away from the chicken pox stricken three-year-old who threatens to interrupt your conversation with his unreasonable demands for pain relief. You will be able to force size six feet into size five shoes. Convince innocent children that not all Mommies are invited to be classroom helpers; it's like a contest you keep losing. Convince yourself that four days in a row of frozen food is really okay for growing children as long as you supplement their diets each morning with a Flintstones vitamin. Sometimes two at a time. Defend yourself against assaults from that most deadly of enemies, the stay-at-home mom, or "The Homers." And that's just home life.

At work, you'll be able to fake reading emails, listening to voice mail, and having a live conversation "over the cube." Most importantly, you'll be able to master the art of making a personal call sound like a work-related call, even when you have to speak the words "runny poo" out loud. You'll have to attempt to hide all traces of a family life that might somehow get in the way of your responsibilities. Particularly from those childless people, or "The Others." Paradoxically, at home, you have to pretend to care about the antics of the fifth grade cut-up your son tells you about each night. And the latest plot on *The Simpsons*. And knowing the Barney birthday song. Here's a tip: young children can often tell when you have on your "faking interest face" far before your colleagues will—if it ever does occur to them. Somehow the detailed data analysis of a direct mail cell is not all that scintillating compared to the aforementioned "runny poo" situation.

So, having it all...be careful what you wish for? The grass is always greener? Blah, blah, blah. The best thing you can do is to appreciate what you have. Look for the quiet times—even if it's only during morning rush hour on the busiest highway in North America—and count each day that doesn't include cleaning up barf as a blessing.

Doing our level best to satisfy our professional and personal needs is the single most important thing that we can do for our employers, and most importantly, our families. We're always going to stumble once in a while: the reports at work will inevitably be turned in late, be incomplete, or be ignored all together, and the children will get yelled at and go out of the house looking like street urchins every once in a while. Use your support system wisely, and don't let your job become an outlet for the stress that you feel at home, and vice versa.

Being a Supermom begins at the moment of conception, and doesn't end unless there's a layoff package. That's from work, not from the child. If you too are in the running for the title of Supermom, I think you'll recognize yourself—my sympathies to you. We're all in this together, so pull up those ripped nylons, force that skirt button to fasten, and march into that office without worrying once about the baby schmutz that's sitting on the right shoulder of your new blazer.

THE SECRET LIFE OF SUPERMOM

Homer: (defn) Interfering individuals, traveling in suburban packs. Known for their ability to watch soap operas while eating bon bons. Seen driving overprotected children to innumerable lessons and play dates. Easily identifiable by their minivans and Gap clothing. Example, Mrs. Kravitz.

Supermom: (defn) Selfish creatures more concerned about not getting jam on their expensive suits than giving little Johnny a hug goodbye in the morning. Easily identifiable by their harried look and inability to find their children's schools on graduation day. Example, Joan Crawford.

Others: (defn) People with lives, i.e. no children. Example, James Bond.

PART 1:

It's Your Basic
Glamour and
Excitement All
the Time, This
Supermom Gig

"Reality is a crutch for people who can't cope with drugs."

—Lily Tomlin

NOW THIS IS WORK!

For a Supermom, a good day is a day when no one throws up on you, splatters food in your face, or calls you a poopyhead. Of course, the fact that you are at work may have something to do with this turn of events, but even then it's not always a sure thing (particularly the name-calling). Yes, we are the Supermoms. Arch enemy of the Homer, alien life form to the Others, and instantly distinguishable by the aura of guilt that surrounds us.

The title of Supermom truly belongs to those who work outside the home, if only in the sense that they take on double duty. The work involved in raising children does not go away during the eight or ten hours one spends at the office. The only piece of work that goes away is the child minding. The laundry, clothes shopping, groceries, cooking, cleaning, guilt, and general stressing are simply packed into a more compact time frame in the evenings and weekends, leaving little or no time for leisure and guilt-free relaxing. Alternatively, having accomplished these Herculean tasks during the workday week, the Homer is more freed up to enjoy the fruits of her labor on the weekend with her partner, versus the "power" grocery shopping Supermom is normally engaged in.

We're not mature enough to allow each of the groups to *celebrate* the lifestyle choices we have made. Instead, we react the way we normally do when we see someone doing something we wouldn't consider doing ourselves: we criticize and we judge.

There is most certainly an animosity that exists between the two groups. The Homers fear the Supermoms have "blown their cover." They have spent years convincing their husband that there is *no way* they could take on a full time job, what with the demands of being a school lunch volunteer, driver for the early band practices, and the after school lessons. Along comes this damn woman who can work and somehow not destine her children towards a career as a psycho killer. The capper on all of this is that these Supermoms then benefit from the poor Homers who have to pick up the slack at school and the associated volunteering duties.

On the other side of the coin, Supermoms look at the Homers with either one or two feelings in mind:

1) Envy—how on earth do these women land husbands who can afford to have a wife at home, and who intellectually support it; or

2) Disbelief—why would you want to subjugate yourself to a man and give your whole life over to your children when everyone knows that all of the studies indicate having a parent at home does not make a significant difference in the child's development?

There is a mutual feeling between the two that the women in the other group are somehow "wasting their time." Either on a career that can't be as important as raising their own children, or on a lifestyle that completely revolves around what the children and the husband expect them to do; paid slavery if you will, to the most cynical. There's a fine line in terms of the appropriate level of involvement in their children's lives. The Homers tend to get more than a little obsessed about the everyday occurrences in their youngster's lives, but more than counterbalance it by genuinely caring about and wanting the best for their children. Problems can arise when they are seen ruthlessly running over other children to get their own child further ahead. Remember the mom who tried to murder her daughter's cheer-leading competition? That lurks in the hearts of more Homers than you care to think about.

Supermoms can't spend as much time with their children as these devoted mothers do, so they're probably not aware of the minutiae in their children's lives, which makes up their successes and challenges. The children would probably like to share this with their Supermom. On the other hand, due to their limited interaction, Supermoms are better able to stand objectively on childhood issues and to sort out the big from the little. It's a fine line, and a fine balance. No one way is the right way. Tip: if you are a Supermom, keep your head down if you have to deal with conflict between your own and a Homer's child. You don't have the time that they do to devote to the case. This is their field of expertise, after all.

Perhaps some of the animosity between the two groups is based on the basic misunderstand-ing of how the others spend their days. For exam-ple, when Supermom takes the day off to spend it with her children it's natural for her to wonder how this day off is any different than *every* day a Homer spends. This could explain some of the friction between the two groups. The Supermom *could* see the Homer as being on a permanent vacation.

Supermom also has to deal with the pressures that come with working in an environment where many of her peers do not understand just how difficult a working mother's life can be. This can cause many moments of frustration for the Supermom. It is fruitless to engage the Others in a discussion about the challenges of attempting to be the Supermom. Just be ready to face some truly grimace-inducing situations. Consider the colleague who states:

"I can hardly get myself ready in the morning. How would I ever get anyone else ready?"

Supermom would be well justified in slapping them. Not that she doesn't believe what the colleague's saying, but it's really a lame platitude. Children force you to do a lot of things, and getting them and yourself out the front door every morning is one of the easy ones.

Here's an even better one:

"I should get time off with pay even though I'm not having any children. I'm tired of supporting other people's selfish childbearing habits."

Fair enough. Take the year off and then cough up the next ten years of daycare and we'll call it even. Take the good, but not the bad. Should everyone who doesn't get married demand a bridal shower for the gifts as well? If you live to be ninety years old, can you demand an early wake so that you can enjoy yourself? If you don't get a terminal disease, can you demand the hospital owes you some free nights and yummy meals in return? Get a grip.

Being at the office when you have children at home is very tough. *Leaving* the office is just as hard. Each day Supermom feels she leaves the office too early, and funnily enough, each day she arrives home too late. This is the curse of the working mother. This is not the curse of the working father. Even the term sounds strange: The working father. Supermom's male colleagues do not suffer from the same afflictions. Perhaps it's hundreds of thousands of years of anthropological training; perhaps it is their inherent belief that it is their right and their privilege to "hunt and gather" outside the home and let the women take on the household. The problem is, Supermom takes on the hunting and gathering too. Does any working father know the last time the children went to the dentist? Their shoe size? Whether they're in the school choir? The last time they had a bath? Dare I say it, their birthdays? How pleasant it must be to be a working father and not have the guilt and stresses that their Supermom counterparts do.

Supermoms make choices to spend time with their children in ways that do not normally occur to their working father peers. Additionally, these choices are often misunderstood even with the best of intentions. Supermoms occasionally venture into the unknown and bravely attempt a field trip. This is the likely scenario:

Teacher: "How nice that you can accompany your child on a trip for once."

Supermom: "Most field trips are announced just days before they are happening, making it extremely difficult for me to attend."

Teacher: "Why?"

Supermom: "Meetings."

(Cue look of disdain from teacher)

Teacher: "Do you mean you would rather attend meetings than go on a school trip with your child?"

Supermoms who attend meeting after meeting know that they would choose bamboo shoots being shoved under their fingernails over attending *another* meeting, let alone use the time to be able to attend a school field trip. There is no suitable reply, given children's ears would be nearby. Upon the Supermom's return to work, coworkers will quiz you as to your absence the day before. If Supermom proudly explains that she has chosen to attend a school field trip (which, by the way, uses up a scarce vacation day), the reply will be an incredulous, "Do you mean you would rather attend a school trip than come into work?"

That's the sound of two worlds colliding.

Any mother (even Homers) will admit that the sight of their children climbing on the school bus and leaving the house for eight hours thrills them. Only the sight of them returning each afternoon matches this thrill. Conflicting emotions are the hallmark of all mothers.

The world that carries on at home does just that even when Supermom is hard at work...well, working. You can be running between meetings when your other life can be thrown at you like a glass of cold water in your face. The call you catch on the last ring prior to it being sentenced to voice mail jail will almost certainly turn out to be the school on the line. Hearts leap to throats. Was one of the children ill? Hurt? In a fight? Usually not.

"Your son has fallen into a mud puddle. Can you please bring him some pants?"

With forced decorum, Supermom must reply politely that as she is at least an hour away, in the middle of a very busy workday, would it be okay, just this once, if the son goes to the lost and found and wears someone else's pants or shorts? The son will think it's cool, and you will have a hard time convincing him to give up the pants he brought home that night. Note to self: stash a spare pair of pants in the eight-year-old's knapsack.

The Ex-Supermom has many similarities with an avid Ex-Smoker. Everything seems brighter, cleaner, and somehow just better once the bad habits of the past have been given up for greener, fresher pastures. Coworkers in their dewy glow of a first maternity leave will gain a new perspective on the old world versus the new.

"I can't believe how I stressed out about work before this baby."

Even the most diligent employee, working long hours to achieve perfection in the imperfect world of business will discover that work stress is a whole different world than growing and forming human life stress. Once the maternity leave is over and she takes on the role of Supermom, she will see how the "real" job begins after the workday ends.

The paradox that evolves is that while the stress of being totally responsible for another human life weighs heavily upon any Mom, Super or otherwise, staying at home with an infant is really *boring. And* the most challenging job in the world. You are not alone, but it is lonely. Any new mother who tells you she is not bored for most of the day when she is alone with her baby is clearly lying. You can only watch them sleep for so long. You will look forward to diaper changing time, feeding time, bathing time, and walk time—it will give you something to do with the hours of tedium. It's almost like sitting through the weekly management meetings at work: taking the minutes, getting the coffee, going to the bathroom *when you don't have to.* You do it just to break up the monotony.

A dichotomy exists when you are the type of woman who honestly enjoys both sides of her life—her professional and her family life. When we're at the office feeling stressed out and under-appreciated, we daydream about blissful days at home with the children. When we're at home with the children, feeling stressed out and unappreciated, we reminisce about the quiet, intellectual times at the office. We want to be in both places at one time, dammit. But only when the times are good in the place that we are in. Get it?

Maternity leaves are a good way for working mothers to experience the stay-at-home lifestyle in an abbreviated and intense fashion. Only the whining, crying, and bodily waste removals break up the endless hours of tedium and boredom. You pray for that moment when "Mr. Wonderful" (and you resent him for *getting* to leave the house each day) is due to come through the front door to save you. There is more work, less sleep, and higher expectations in a very short time period. Which is more annoying? The husband who comes home after work and states "Who made this mess?" and proceeds to clean up the offending materials, or the husband who ignores the mess and doesn't help to clean up at all? Either way, he's just wrong. Supermoms leave the house for a few hours here and there, and come home either to no household chores being done in their absence or to a spotless kitchen with a sleeping baby. Which is more irksome? A husband with the ability to get things done with a newborn on-site, or a husband who is virtually unable to get a single thing done? Either way, he loses.

Each night during a maternity leave, Supermom will dream about the freedom of the next day—no deadline, phone calls, or emails, just the notion of puttering around the house with her sweet baby. Nine o'clock the next morning, however, you can find her emailing friends, making half a dozen phone calls, and setting up appointments with precision deadlines. Old habits die hard. There are days when Supermom longs for an in-box and the goodies that come inside. Everyone needs to feel needed, organized, and important. It's hard to feel this way when you've got a streak of baby poop up one arm, a four-year-old drawing on the wall with your lipstick, and the sound of glass gently breaking from the basement below.

By definition, most of us haven't gotten the title of "Mommy" without some help. So let's go to the husbands. Where are they in all of this guilt and confusion and what the hell are they doing about it? Contrary to public opinion, they're not useless at all things; they're just mostly useless in the home. How many men do you know who refer to spending time with their own children (while mother is out) as "babysitting"? Men feel an inherent right of freedom to disappear to the washroom for two hours, spend thirty minutes tinkering with a latch on their car door, ten minutes hosing down the driveway, or numerous other seemingly harmless but time-consuming tasks. They do not feel the same compulsion that women do to announce to their spouse that they will not be "in charge" of watching the children while they perform these tasks. Personally, I advise my husband when I will be taking a thirty-second pee. "Are you watching them? Do you know where they are?" I'll cry as I zip by him. If I receive a grunt in reply, I go for it, relishing my quick parole. To paraphrase Henry Higgins, "Why can't a man be more like a woman?"

A GUIDE FOR SPOTTING THE DIFFERENCES BETWEEN HOMERS AND SUPERMOMS

Homer	Supermom
Watches daytime talk shows religiously; unusual not to sob openly at least once during each show.	Can't watch daytime talk show for more than five minutes before yelling out loud at the women on the show to "get a life."
Believes if she misses one episode of her soap opera she will never catch up.	Can miss two years' worth and return comfortably to the same storyline.

Homer	Supermom
Welcomes bake sale days at the school.	Worries about getting to the twenty-four-hour grocery store in time, morning of.
Knows precisely what the baby has eaten during the day, when the last nap was taken, and the amount of waste that's been discharged.	Remembers to pick up kids on time.
Feels that school drop-off and pick-up is a stressful complication on the way to tennis.	Feels that school drop-off and pick-up is a stressful complication on the way to the office.
Worships at the shrine of Dr. Phil.	Worships at the shrine of Allison Pearson.

Homer	Supermom
Irons everything, from children's pajamas to drapes to husband's shirts.	Uses the iron as the heavy thing to balance out the shelf in the laundry room.
Spends hours each week in cold, damp hockey arenas encouraging young prodigy and berating volunteer coaches and referees.	Pretends that hockey doesn't exist.
Washes linens at least once a week.	Changes the pillow-cases when the sleep drool begins to smell.
Completely conver-sant in children's school lessons, including homework assignments, topics covered in social his-tory, and the smallest detail of the teacher's personal life.	They take something called social history?

Homer	Supermom
Expert at building pyramids out of Play-Doh, wind tunnels out of toilet paper rolls, and topographic maps out of paper mâche.	"It's your homework, not mine."
Pizza lunch monitor extraordinaire.	What time is the lunch break?
Witnesses children as leads in school plays, soloists in school choir, school bus patrollers, hall monitors firsthand, as she spends all of her free time volunteering at the school.	Makes it to the school concert, albeit in the last row. Child is often not actually seen performing due to last row status.
Can't wait for summer breaks to spend more quality time with her children, and sleep in until 10:00 a.m.	Starts summer break planning in January, in order to secure day camp placement the minute school ends in June.

Homer	Supermom
Serves as chairperson at all school fundraisers, fun fairs, concerts, etc.	Considers it a great accomplishment to show up.
Finds hats and mittens for first cold day of school, forty-three days before it happens, and then has them "at the ready."	"Don't be such a wimp. Pull your hood over your head and your arms up your coatsleeves to keep your hands warm."
Picks up children every day at school to ferry them home for a hot, nutritional lunch in calm and pleasant surroundings.	Feels virtuous when a piece of fruit gets put in the plastic lunch bag along with the leftover pizza and Twinkies.

Homer	Supermom
Notices when other neighbors have guests staying, work being done, change in working hours, husband working late repeatedly, vacation absences.	Wouldn't blink an eye if two men with an unmarked van suspiciously emptied the neighbor's house while they were on vacation.

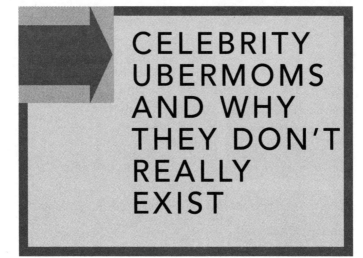

CELEBRITY UBERMOMS AND WHY THEY DON'T REALLY EXIST

Come on, we were all excited when Kate Hudson got really fat while expecting her first child. Unfortunately now she's skinny again, and most Supermoms are still working off the last ten pounds from a child we gave birth to five years ago, not five months ago. Gwyneth Paltrow thinks women should stay at home with their children. Skinny rich cow. If someone would pay this Supermom eight million dollars for one kick-ass business case, I'd retire too. Then there's Elizabeth Hurley and her flat stomach scant moments after giving birth, nuzzling her Little Precious as she strolls through Heathrow Airport in a spotless all-white outfit, completely perfect and pristine after a twelve-hour flight. No leaky diapers and poop stains for this Ubermom. No all-over massive body-sweats and frighteningly large hair losses months after the birth. This baby has been seemingly plucked cleanly from her body without leaving behind even a trace of his former living arrangements. Ms. Hurley reportedly hid out at Elton John's mansion, worked out for two to three hours a day, and lived on only brown rice and watercress soup for seven weeks. Miraculously, she shed the fifty-three pounds she supposedly gained during her pregnancy (which probably landed her at a hefty 130 at the height of her weight gain). How wonderful it would be to hang out at a rich guy's mansion, with loads of staff that will watch the baby, feed the baby, and change the baby, etc., while we work out all afternoon. Shit, *most* Supermoms would work out for five hours if this were the setup. She admits that her main motivation was money. Her income is directly linked to her looks. Unfortunately, or fortunately, this is not the case for most Supermoms. Very unfortunately, we are constantly judged by the unreasonable standards set by these Uberbitches.

Think for a minute about the hardest part of having a baby. It's not the pregnancy, labor, delivery, or in some cases, even the conception. It's the preconceived expectations of being able to bounce back into your pre-pregnancy jeans a few days after giving birth. Even Supermom can't overcome the lack of sleep in those first few weeks and find the energy to work on improving herself. It's no surprise that sleep deprivation is used as a form of torture. It is torture. Real Supermoms have been known to stagger through the streets shooting venomous looks at everyone they pass, madly thinking to themselves that they would bet their child's life everyone else has gotten more sleep than them, and they absolutely hate them for it. This is the key element that is missing from the Ubermom's new parenting lifestyle. Not that they have people to sleep for them (although if such a thing could be purchased, it would be), rather that they have people to *allow* them to sleep, thus giving them the opportunity to regain their humanlike qualities.

Glossy American soap opera episodes normally include a woman waking up in full makeup, children who age ten years overnight, and evil twins who pop up from the dead. We can take all of this. It's fantasy. However, they push it too far when they show a mother who has given birth only two weeks prior fitting back into her size zero spaghetti-strap dress, working silently in her beautifully decorated office. What's so strange about that? The baby is with her *at the office*, in a bassinet. Ubermom is able to take meetings, read, size up new hunks, discuss complicated plot elements with other characters, all while the baby sleeps or plays quietly in its cot, dressed in starched white linens. Unless her meetings, stud drooling, and relationship therapy could have taken place within a twenty-seven-second period, this scene is totally ridiculous. Normal attempts to work at home are so disastrous that often subterfuge is required (i.e. curtains on the home office glass door) to convince offspring that you have left the premises.

Even Supermom can't expect to live up to these fantasies, yet subconsciously, perhaps we expect that she *should*. Compare yourself to your truly imperfect peers only. For the record, Kelly Ripa is a freak of nature. And just remember—you didn't look like Elizabeth Hurley prior to having a baby, please don't expect to resemble her *after*.

There is one tip about weight loss that we can take from these Ubermoms. Some of the hardest, fittest bodies in the world are endorsing this new fabulous method of losing weight and toning up. Pamela Anderson, Demi Moore, Elle MacPherson, and Cindy Crawford all swear by it. Catherine Zeta-Jones endorses it in every post-baby interview she gives. The secret? You can lose weight and look great by...*running after your own children.* Just ask them. All along we had been led to believe that having children made you gain weight and get soft. Apparently not. These women maintain that they eat "normally" and that they don't have any special exercise routine at all.

"Well, I have three children, you know," forty-something Demi responded in an interview. "That'll keep anyone in shape." She did admit to one more secret, which is that she "moved furniture around her house, a lot." This Supermom could push a couch up four flights of stairs twelve times a day and not look like her. All of those reports on her spending $400,000 on plastic surgery were apparently vicious rumors. This could be good news for some Supermoms. You might not have $400,000, but you might have something better. *Four* children (like me). I could beat those skinny amateurs who only had two or three children.

Here is the plan.

Day One: A rainy day calls for an indoor playground. Visualize the inches whittling away as you dash around the indoor playground, laughing and chatting with the other svelte mothers. Just pay the woman, finish your coffee, and then zip off after them.

(Not surprisingly, these playgrounds are stocked with the latest celebrity gossip magazines. Given that these people are to be your role model in your new-body quest, you should feel obliged to read about their goings on.)

One hour later, the kids are exhausted and your only movement is likely to have been from the couch to the ball pit to advise the four-year-old about the "no balls to the head" rule. Do note the surprising amount of chubby women in the playground. They too may have just started on their new quest.

One month later: You may start to suspect that there's a crack in the diet philosophy of the thin, fit celebrity crowd. Most of the women in the real world are struggling with their weight even with a gaggle of children to chase after. Clothes keep getting tighter, not looser. And, while the pounds are being put on while in pursuit of my children, these famously sleek women have gotten thinner, tighter, and maybe even younger.

The grim reality that they had probably been lying to elevate themselves to that even more enviable state of thin: That of being effortlessly so.

These women just look tighter than their former "loose" selves did. They have been tweaked by some of the best surgeons and personal trainers that money can buy, not by chasing their soon-to-be-arrested-for-underage-drinking-and-internet-sex-tapes-children. Frivolous surgery really is the only way to look that good.

We will have to undo the damage that Pamela, Demi, and the rest of them have purposefully done to us real Supermoms running after children. The worse *we* look, the better *they* look. They are professionals at self-elevation. Ms. Zeta-Jones did not marry Michael Douglas for his money and fame, but for the fact that she will always look young in his company. How long has that woman been 34, anyway?

Whatever *their* reality, *our* reality is that it is only going to be exercise and food control that will unbloat our bodies from their childbearing shapes. Dammit.

The moral of the story is that, unless "running after your children" literally means you are the full-time coach of your son the Olympic cross country star, you will not be able to attain the ideal pinup girl shape in this way. (Too bad, as I was thinking of having a fifth just to improve my odds.)

SLEEP? I DON'T NEED NO STINKING SLEEP...

Yes, you do. Supermom or not, without sleep we're pretty crabby and stunned. Potentially hundreds of extremely bad business strategies have been moved forward simply because Supermom is being bitchy-scary at work. There is absolutely nothing that can prepare you for the first few months of your newborn's life in terms of sleep deprivation. But you will get through it. We wander through our days a little dazed and confused, but still giddy in the knowledge that we have a beautiful baby to show for our efforts. Our bodies are healing and our lack of sleep is a badge of honor.

Listen in on a group of new parents, and I guarantee you the first thing they'll talk about (after the grisly birth details) is how long Little Precious slept the previous night. It will quickly degenerate into a contest whereby the winner is either the one with the least sleep, or, strangely, the most. It's truly a beautiful thing when they finally sleep through the night—and *really* through the night (i.e. 8:00 p.m. to at least 7:00 a.m.). Many first-timers will try to pass off a stint of 12:00 midnight to 4:00 a.m. as "through the night."

Once the newborn has passed into the blissful stage of seven, eight, nine hours of sleep or more, you start to feel human again. This can be short-lived if the teething stage sets in shortly after, but remember that this too will pass. Remember when your biggest challenge was getting to work on time? On a full night's sleep?

There are a significant amount of Supermoms whose children are well past the newborn stage—up to six years old in some cases—and are still not sleeping through the night. Could some of it be Supermom's fault? Supermoms can be guilty of prolonging this due to their own feelings of guilt over "abandoning" the needs of their baby during the day (an activity otherwise known as earning a paycheck).

"But he needs me to sleep with him. I had to buy a new double bed just so we could share."

How does Supermom expect this to end? With the two-year-old finally sitting down with Mom and saying "I'm okay now, Mom, you can go and join Dad"? Never going to happen. The worst culprit is the parent who allows her child to get into her bed night after night, *when the mom doesn't want the child to be there.* This is not the place for a public forum on the Family Bed, although there can't be a more torturous sleeping condition. No, this refers to the folks who *complain* about their children getting in their bed and *still allow them to do* it night after night. The best solution is to lead them back to their bed and immediately return to yours. An intermediary step (if the best solution is too harsh and the child is hysterical) is to lie down with them in *their* bed, not yours. This way they will learn that their own bed is a safe place, and that Mommy and Daddy's bed is not their bed.

Having just spent a sleepless night due to my four-year-old's middle of the night wanderings, I know firsthand that the best intentions can go awry. The key here is perseverance. Don't do anything you do not want to repeat 100 times. Take them back to their bed. Again and again. They will get it. I think it's a good idea to state your expectations to your children when you put them to bed. For example, "I expect you to stay in bed all night."

That's it. Then you can have a similar discussion the next morning, and the next evening, to explain why Mommy is so upset (and scary-looking too) when they are up in the night. Children are smarter than we think and, until they reach puberty, they are very motivated to make Mom or Dad happy. They want to be liked, just like the rest of us.

So go ahead and feel selfish about getting sleep. Don't feel guilty about banishing them to their beautifully furnished, Disney-linened, well-ventilated bedrooms. They will survive, and you'll be a better parent in the morning because of it. You might still be scary-looking, but what Supermom isn't at 6:00 a.m.?

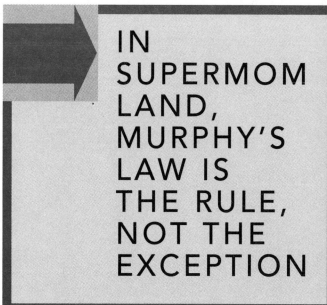

IN SUPERMOM LAND, MURPHY'S LAW IS THE RULE, NOT THE EXCEPTION

Murphy's Law—that things will go wrong at precisely the moment you need them to go right—is prevalent in every mother's life, and magnified even more so for Supermom. Children never get sick until your husband is out of town and you have a huge presentation to give to the senior executive team. *"Why did they have to pick today?"* And you're speaking about the kids getting sick, not the presentation scheduler.

School concerts or plays will be held on evenings when you or your spouse absolutely has to be out of town on business, leaving the other to make excuses and wrangle all of the other children to the overcrowded gym.

The car will run out of gas when you have to pick up the kids, get to an important meeting, and make it to your thrice rescheduled doctor's appointment, the sole purpose of which is to acquire a new prescription for birth control pills.

You only find a good, close parking space at the mall when you *don't* have all of your children in tow, and it's not raining, snowing, or windy.

You'll *always* get a bad haircut just days before the annual dinner dance for your husband's company. It doesn't seem to happen days before your own, where people already know you and know that you can pull off looking good when you really try. It only happens with strangers who've speculated as to what you look like. You'll give them something to talk about for weeks.

You'll run into old acquaintances, particularly the male ones, when you've zipped out without combing your hair, putting on lipstick, and are wearing that pair of pants you really hate but can't get rid of because you need them at the end of every week when the laundry is behind.

You will *always* get your period the day before: a) the annually scheduled bikini wax, b) a day at the beach with your in-laws, or c) the night you have promised your sex-starved husband that this will be the one night this month he is really going to be glad he waited.

A nosy neighbor (usually a well-organized Homer) will visit when you've staged a revolt against the children by not picking up their errant jackets, boots, and knapsacks from the front door. The phone will only ring when you're having a heart-to-heart conversation with your children or your husband, not when you're trying to get rid of above nosy neighbor. The baby will scream during a conference call at home, while the three-year-old will have gotten her head stuck between the stair railings.

You'll get pregnant when you're not trying. Babies will only spit up on you when you either have an expensive shirt on or are in a place where you cannot change into anything else. Ditto on the explosive bowel movements.

You will finally get around to reading a book like this and you will already know everything in it.

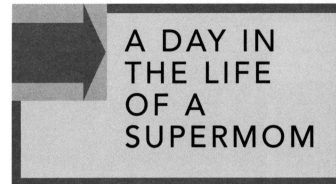

A DAY IN THE LIFE OF A SUPERMOM

F ace it. Many of your compatriots at work have no idea what your day is really like. When you mention to them that your "real work day" starts when you arrive home at night, they will smirk. They'll be thinking that in *their* opinion, you get in late and you leave early, every single day. So you have to put a couple of kids to bed when you get home. What could be so tough about that?

4:30 a.m. Awake to cries of teething eight-month-old baby. Marvel at and admire husband's ability to sleep through cacophony, when slightest noise made by children during the History Channel's *1000 Great War Moments* can cause the 1001st moment in your own home.

4:46 a.m. Drift back to sleep after having groped halfway downstairs in the dark to find a missing pacifier for baby, only to discover it wedged between two of your toes. Pull pacifier out, return to nursery, and pop into baby's mouth.

4:51 a.m. Awake to noise of three-year-old who has decided now is the perfect time to dump all of the hard plastic bath toys into the ceramic tub and look for her favorite plastic soap dish. Scuttle her into your bed with evil thoughts of waking Sir Sleepalot in the space next to you.

5:30 a.m. Hit alarm button and remove the three-year-old's heel from deep within your rib cage. Awaken husband with a gentle "You want the shower first, move it!"

6:15 a.m. Remind husband that every minute spent sitting on the toilet reading could be a minute spent getting ready or bonding with his children.

6:30 a.m. Finish world's quickest shower and grope through underwear drawer for a pair still sporting working elastic. Decide that the maternity pair will do, and then be suitably mortified at their excellent fit.

6:35 a.m. Scour closet for one clean blouse and a jacket long enough to hide top of pants to leave button undone, should the need arise. Answer "Yes!" to husband's question of "Does this match?" in reference to his own ensemble. Save "Are you really wearing that?" remark until he's walking out the door, just to be cute. Listen for baby on monitor and try to hide disappointment that he will be spending another minute in slumber, instead of with you.

6:45 a.m. In your best indoor voice, advise older children of the need to arise from their bedchambers and to prepare themselves for a day of learning.

6:50 a.m. Advise in a firm voice that time is ticking away and they'll miss the bus if they don't get a move on.

7:00 a.m. Threaten boarding school. Voice level adjustable.

7:15 a.m. Prepare children's lunches while reading crumpled notes from teacher, pulled from depths of scary knapsacks. Have moral moment while trying to decide whether to admit to noticing the "cupcake day" flyer that clearly states that today is the day. Get caught with notice in hand by son who apologizes and then offers to help make twelve cupcakes before school. Remind him of the twenty four-hour supermarket at the end of the street. Curtail any further discussion about the "fun" of making them together, with just one glance. Glance at still-silent baby monitor and sigh wistfully.

7:20 a.m. Empty dishwasher, while taking a moment of thanks that no one else has discovered your surreptitious behavior, which allows them to continue their belief in the dishwasher fairy, who likely cohabitates with the toilet paper replacement fairy.

7:30 a.m. Finish assembling children's lunches, with fervent hope that a wonderful stay-at-home mother isn't volunteering at your children's lunch table to witness the leftover pate, chocolate cheesecake, and an apple with one bite taken out of it. Oh, and the grape soda as well. Out of orange juice.

7:45 a.m. Lay out children's belongings for school, including knapsacks, mittens (matching ones are so formal), hats, coats, boots, gym clothes, and signed teachers' notes. Take a moment to inquire of husband as to whether he needs any help "getting himself together." Admire him sashaying out the front door. Remind him that you will show the baby his picture in order to keep the familiarity intact. Glance at still-silent baby monitor in disgust.

7:58 a.m. Peek furtively out window in hopes that nanny will one day appear two minutes early instead of two minutes late. Suddenly remember that batteries for baby monitor were taken out by nine-year-old son for latest electronic game. Race upstairs to confront red-faced angry infant who will no doubt relive this event in future therapy sessions.

8:02 a.m. Call down to nanny "I'm changing a diaper here!" while grappling with the remnants of baby's first effort at eating smoked fish. Pray to any and all gods that she will take the hint and come up to reprieve you and your suit.

8:06 a.m. Struggle downstairs with screaming baby and ignore nanny's doubtful look as you advise that baby has had a little sleep-in, but is now hungry for his breakfast. Pretend not to hear the under-the-breath remark of "babies need schedules."

8:10 a.m. Step outside the door and chuckle to self at blue tights now evident under the black skirt. Zip back inside to pull on longest boots. Yell to son that you'll bring double the amount of cupcakes to the school next month.

8:15 a.m. Get on cell phone to check messages and have second moral moment of day while trying to decide whether to admit receipt of message from boss advising of 7:00 a.m. emergency meeting that morning. Message left last night at 5:01, one minute after all thoughts of work had left head. Decide to blame voice mail system for delivery problems.

8:20 a.m. Still in traffic. Worry about dinner.

8:30 a.m. Still in traffic. Worry about weight.

8:40 a.m. Still in traffic. Decide on fat-free dinner.

8:50 a.m. Still in traffic. After searching mind, discover lack of knowledge of any fat-free dinners.

9:00 a.m. Still in traffic, office in sight. Decide dinner is husband's problem tonight.

9:10 a.m. Arrive breathless in office and race into management meeting pretending to be only ten minutes late, instead of two hours. Still offer up, "Did I miss anything?"

9:30 a.m. Should have stopped for a coffee since late anyway.

9:59 a.m. Count 817 ceiling tiles in this meeting room. Skirt is killing me. These people are really annoying. And ugly.

10:02 a.m. Glance anxiously at watch every ten seconds as a reminder to others that meeting is running over time.

10:12 a.m. Call son's teacher twelve minutes late for scheduled teleconference, and apologize profusely. Remain silent when told of "mooning" incident. Re-avow to spend more time reminding child of school behavior rules.

10:17 a.m. Berate self for bad parenting.

10:19 a.m. Assign half of blame to child's father.

10:29 a.m. Slop coffee on self while running to meeting thirteen floors away. Send up useless prayer to any god that the suit jacket will button up for the first time in six-and-a-half years, in order to cover stain.

10:30 a.m. Continue blasphemous streak.

10:32 a.m. Race into meeting late, apologizing profusely for delay. Spill coffee on colleague while trying to unobtrusively find place at overcrowded boardroom table.

10:35 a.m. Give superior smirk to a late arrival at meeting, glancing at watch to emphasize the inappropriateness of that behavior.

11:27 a.m. Finish writing grocery list and start composing wedding speech for brother's upcoming nuptials.

11:28 a.m. Nod knowingly at colleague's comments and madly scramble mentally to tune into discussion prior to opinion being sought.

11:29 a.m. Feign interest in outcome of research findings.

11:46 a.m. Cough loudly to suppress growling stomach and check agenda to ensure lunch is part of the program.

11:47 a.m. Curse "Cost Containment—We All Need to Pitch In" program while reading note on meeting agenda reminding attendees of the "bag it and bring it" policy. Check meeting end time. Groan audibly as cafeteria closes at 2:00.

2:01 p.m. Realize more than two hours have passed and there is no recollection of any details from the meeting whatsoever, besides the fact that cafeteria closing time has come and gone.

2:06 p.m. On way back to veal-fattening pen cubicle, stuff staff suggestion box with "Nap Room" recommendation yet one more time.

2:08 p.m. Begin listening to eighteen voice messages. Skip all those except from boss, nanny, and husband. On second thought, skip those from husband.

2:26 p.m. Begin returning first of one hundred and three new messages in email, vowing once again to ban the "reply all" command from staff's computers.

2:28 p.m. Feign interest in colleague's photos of new dog while returning emails and tapping foot violently against chair leg.

2:35 p.m. Visit office newsstand for new pair of pantyhose, reminding self to trade chair for one which doesn't snack on nylon. Target a subordinate's cubicle when no one is looking.

2:36 p.m. Get caught by Executive Vice President at office newsstand, while noting that own self is running late for quarterly EVP update in boardroom. Sneak chocolate bar and soda onto the magazine rack and hold up pantyhose as acceptable excuse for lateness. Belatedly realize sixty-two-year-old men could misinterpret this gesture.

2:45 p.m. Enter boardroom late and with legs held tightly together due to misunderstanding of sizing on pantyhose label. Try to look on bright side, as six-year-old daughter could use new pair of tights.

4:12 p.m. Catch head rolling backwards in nick of time and join in healthy applause at end of endless session. Because it's over.

4:17 p.m. Begin returning emails, voice mails, snail mails, and glance at little sticky notes stuck to computer in case they contain good office gossip.

4:58 p.m. Realize time and hastily begin packing away papers and frantically searching for shoes under desk. Hear voices approaching and consider launching self under desk to avoid interaction.

5:04 p.m. Explain for fourteenth time that you cannot be late and push elevator button frantically, while ducking head to avoid eye contact with EVP getting off alternate elevator.

5:07 p.m. Stop at newsstand for sustenance (i.e. chocolate bar) to eat on way home. Get stuck behind little Miss Office Organizer buying eighteen different types of lottery tickets, with funds taken out of eighteen different envelopes. Hope she wins so you don't have to see her again.

5:18 p.m. Run through parking lot, dodging approaching cars, trying to make up every minute. Ignore pantyhose now down around ankles.

5:47 p.m. After sitting for ten minutes in same spot on highway, start to feel a little panicky about being home on time.

5:49 p.m. Begin outwardly cursing and berating other drivers.

5:51 p.m. Start to dial husband to find out if his estimated time of arrival can be moved up. At the last minute remember he has a team bonding night booked and won't be home until later that evening, when the hellish tide of bedtimes has ended.

5:59 p.m. Phone nanny to explain only ten minutes away, at most.

6:11 p.m. Hope God doesn't punish liars.

6:22 p.m. Quietly open door and announce arrival, secretly praying that all children have mysteriously developed sleeping disease and are at peace in bed. Have guilty moment.

6:23 p.m. Embrace children who are happy to see you (i.e. those under the age of five), and advise older children, in response to their question, that dinner will be a "surprise!" (To you as well.)

6:25 p.m. After emitting several hundred apologies to nanny, realize have promised her an afternoon off in return for her twenty two-minute delay this evening. Vow to worry about that another time.

6:26 p.m. Stare into refrigerator hoping something will transpire, while simultaneously attempting to open baby food jar and clean up spilled chocolate milk.

6:30 p.m. Get frozen lasagna out of wrapper and into oven. Make potential health-damaging decision on healthiness of wilting carrots and rotting cucumber. Decide roughage can come from breakfast next morning.

7:20 p.m. Dinner on the table to groans and moans of ungrateful children, punctuated by the pre-teen vegan wannabe wailing about the unfairness of it all. Boldly lie and state that it is a vegetarian lasagna and that the beef is really tofu.

7:21 p.m. Truth about meat is relayed to vegan sister by carnivore brother. Swear that both of them will be eating nothing but dry toast for the next two weeks, and then realize that type of reward is not in order.

7:25 p.m. Survey tomato sauce and cheese artwork deposited on floor under three-year-old's chair, and wonder if four days (until the cleaning lady comes) is too long to leave it. Decision made by baby spitting up all over dry-clean only blouse. The food stays.

8:00 p.m. Deposit baby into crib after cleaning up Poo Festival 2005. Whose idea was the white carpet in the nursery? Make note to buy area rug.

8:13 p.m. Continue with harassment of school-age children over homework. Calmly state that you could do it for them, but it's not for you to learn. Pray they take this as an answer to avoid revealing lack of knowledge of the mottoes of each state.

8:30 p.m. Drag screaming three-year-old out of the basement to be taken upstairs to bed. Reach upstairs bathroom and embrace Poo Festival, The Reunion, prior to a hasty tooth brushing. It's more important they eat fruit than get a good scrub.

8:35 p.m. Put laundry in to ensure daughter's only white shirt is clean for band performance tomorrow. Chuckle at the irony of having missed the pink lip gloss in her shirt pocket and attempt the bleaching process.

9:00 p.m. Ensure older children are in rooms, reading suitable material. Review daughter's instant messaging conversation which has been left on the computer and decide it's probably just as well you can't understand the abbreviations.

9:30 p.m. Go through own closet to find a too-small white shirt that will fit daughter.

10:00 p.m. Crawl into bed to hear door lock, announcing husband's return to the home front. Decide on silent approach when greeted with, "Must be nice to get to bed so early. Quiet evening? My day was hell, I can tell you. Did you pick up my shirts from the dry cleaners? I'm fresh out, you know."

10:03 p.m. Use withholding sex as a weapon. Again. Look forward to a fresh start in the morning.

2:06 a.m. Is it morning already? In this house it is, or so the baby has announced. Here we go again. And it's karate lessons tonight...

SUPERMOM— BEHIND CLOSED DOORS

There are days when a Supermom can convince herself she really does have it all together. The sun is shining, the house is clean (or you are of the frame of mind to overlook the dust and dirt) and the kids aren't getting on your nerves. Not that the children are actually behaving, they're just not annoying you. Children are always behaving in one way or another—good, bad, horrible, angelic. It's all a stage performance to some degree. So is most mothering. In this era of reality television, imagine what would be captured if a film crew followed the average Supermom around. Some of it wouldn't be pretty, I assure you.

They would witness the times you wipe up spills on the kitchen floor with your stocking feet, instead of reaching down with a wet cloth. Even if it's red juice. Even if you're wearing white socks.

What about the amount of food slurped from the saucepans while making dinner, without washing the spoon clean in between? Hey, you all have the same genes so you can share the germs, too. You just don't want those people licking *your* spoon.

Then there's the amount of precious artwork one throws out on a daily basis. There's only so much of this stuff you can keep. Really. And not all of it is very good. Really.

Supermoms can get quite good at denying eating their daughter's chocolate bar and letting her pin it on her younger brother. It's something he *would* do, if he had the chance, so he can take the blame once in a while. He's probably gotten away with something else this week.

There are nights when Supermom will secretly pray that their eldest child will keep her light on just a bit too long reading, so you can legitimately state to your husband that it is too late to engage in any hanky-panky. Just a few nights to yourself, okay?

Supermom can admit to letting the children eat in the family room to avoid a fight, and then giving them a stern look when their father discovers gooey marshmallow all over the carpet. Silently nodding your head in agreement with him when he restates the "no food in the family room" rule yet again.

You can exaggerate the number of times you get up during the night with the baby just so your husband will feel guilty the next night and do double duty. (A bad idea if hubby is a light sleeper and can count.)

Supermoms often count the minutes until the children's bedtime and then gaze at them adoringly when they're asleep, wishing them to wake up again.

You stick your finger into the children's food to make sure that it's hot or cold enough and then lick it off.

Drink Diet Pepsi for breakfast to get a caffeine jolt without having to go to the trouble of making coffee, but disguise it from the children by putting it into a mug.

Supermoms live in a paradoxical world of sorts, swinging from the kindest human being your children know—the mother who lets them eat cookies for breakfast, just this once—to the meanest, crankiest soul they've ever come across when they attempt to take advantage the next morning. That's how it must seem to them. We have many sides to our personalities, and many of them are facades which may appear at any one time.

The Supermom needs to let her guard down once in a while, and most often that will be when she's at home alone. So eat those stolen chocolate bars, buy a trashy magazine every once in a while, and sometimes just do what makes you feel good for the moment. You need it, and you deserve it. Just don't get caught.

YOU THINK POOPY DIAPERS ARE BAD...

Supermom Scenario: You're out visiting, and naturally, your little angel has a "filler" in his diaper. As you kneel on the floor, changing a diaper with one hand, drinking coffee with the other, you continue to carry on a conversation. If the person to whom you are speaking does not have any children, (this will become apparent by the growing look of horror on their face due to their closest encounter with baby shit), they are likely to blurt out, "Oh, I don't know how you can do that. Changing diapers must be just the worst thing!"

Cue Supermom explosive laughter. Changing diapers, for the uninitiated, is a minor incident in the caring and feeding for your baby. People have been known to extend the years their child is in a diaper just to avoid the trauma and tribulations of toilet training and the unspeakable fear you have when your three-year-old is in thin, cotton, unabsorbent underwear. Changing diapers is like breathing when you have a child. You almost forget you're doing it. Except, of course, when the urine or poo ends up in places where it shouldn't be—like on your blouse, under your fingernails, or on a new carpet.

What's the "worst" thing a Supermom has to worry about? Diapers would probably come in at about number thirty-six...

1) Death. Stressing almost every minute of every day about somebody dying. They die and you live. You die and they live. Your husband dies and you and the children both live. Stop thinking about it.

2) Injury. Watching them take those first few steps across the living room floor, knowing that they're going to crack their head on the edge of the babyproofed fireplace, making you the first person ever to sue the childproofing company for faulty products.

3) Sleep. The total lack of sleep in the first few weeks or months, and then never getting to have as deep a sleep ever again once a child is in your life. You will hear every cough, movement, and whimper (note this section for *mothers* only).

4) Development. "Developmentally delayed" are the worst words you can think of when it comes to your children. Not sitting up when they're "supposed to." Crawling late, walking late, talking late, never crawling, too many temper tantrums.

5) Nutrition. Are they eating enough of the right foods? Drinking enough of the right drinks? Are they too skinny? Too fat? Healthy? Unhealthy? Allergic? Drunk?

6) Intelligence. Are they destined for manual labor? Because they can't spell their name by the end of kindergarten, does this signal lifelong failure? Especially when their name is Al?

7) Social acceptability. Do they have friends? Enough friends? The right friends? Do the friends have the right parents? Do you like the parents? Do you have to like the parents? Are your children ugly? Nerdy? Jerks? It's hard to tell sometimes.

8) Competitiveness. Are they in the right lessons? Do they know the right teachers? Have you been pushing them hard enough? Too hard? Do they work hard enough at their homework? Do *you* work hard enough at their homework?

9) Cleanliness. Besides first-time parents, most people bathe their children only once or twice a week, right? I remember my daughter at the age of six being upset because someone at school said

her hair "stinks." I thought to myself "well, does it?" I checked, and *that* day, it didn't.

10) Social responsibility. Do they know right from wrong? Do they care? Are they likely to be too wild? Too prudish? Too slutty? Too goody-two-shoes? Which way should we lean in terms of pushing them one way or another? Do we encourage them to date? To use condoms? Ugh.

11) Guilt. Would they be this socially annoying if you didn't work? Would their attitudes toward food and cleanliness be healthier if you didn't buy fast food and hire a cleaning lady?

As the saying goes, "Little children, little problems. Big children, big problems." Changing diapers is such a little problem in the pursuit of raising a happy, healthy, successful child. It's one of the easiest messes to clean up. Bail is harder.

TIMES WHEN YOU REALLY DON'T FEEL LIKE SUPERMOM

1) Ten seconds after you've just yelled at your kids. If it was a minor infraction, you'll feel you overreacted. If it was for a big thing, you'll feel that ultimately it is your fault, not theirs, as you must have done such a lousy job raising them. If only you didn't work, they'd be perfect.

2) You send your kids to school without a hat or gloves. Not because it's not cold—it is—but because you can't find them and you don't have the time to look any further. Then you feel terrible again, when you realize that at the end of the workday you haven't given this particular situation a second thought.

3) You're excited when you get to leave the house without them. And when you come home to a quiet house after a late meeting, you're grateful that you don't have to deal with them again until the morning.

4) They ask for an apple for their snack and you offer a cookie instead, because you forgot to buy fruit when grocery shopping. Okay, you forgot to grocery shop entirely. For extra points, the next time they ask for a cookie, you say, "Have an apple!"

5) You have them pull a dirty shirt out of the laundry because you're so far behind in the wash they have nothing else to wear. You blame them for growing so quickly that hardly any of their clothes purchased two years ago don't fit anymore.

6) You know the car seat isn't tethered in correctly, and you still take them out in the car. Or worse, you realize when you get home from a forty-five-minute drive that you haven't buckled them in at all.

7) You feed a newborn formula that's been sitting out for more than an hour and they throw it all up two minutes later. You then complain about the barf to your partner when he comes home. "He just can't keep anything down today. You deal with him, I've had it."

8) Your child says, "I don't like you anymore. You're not my friend." You'll bend over backwards for the next fifteen minutes after that one, trying to prove to a two-year-old that you are worth having for a friend.

9) You find yourself saying, "Well, sometimes I don't like you either." And you really mean it. For five seconds.

10) They want you to watch them do something totally inane, and you tell them you don't have time for that sort of thing. The guilt is compounded when they tell their friends, "My mom isn't interested in watching me practice being a rock for the school play. I doubt she'll even come."

11) They want to do arts and crafts with you, and you tell them it would be better if they watched another hour of television. Eventually you relent, and then curse them five minutes later when the paint, water, and glue is spilled all over the distressed oak dining table.

12) You threaten to tell Santa they've been bad. In your head, you also threaten to tell them Santa doesn't exist.

13) You send them to school when they complain of a sore stomach, fever, or headache. Your plans for the day are ultimately ruined at any rate when you have to leave the office to go to the

school and pick them up, studiously avoiding the janitor who has been working for hours to clean up their trail of vomit.

14) When they hear you mutter under your breath "I can't wait to get to work," and you're glad they did.

KETCHUP *IS* A VEGETABLE IN MY HOUSE

Reportedly there has been a recent surge in cookbook sales. Not because more of us are actually cooking, but we're using the cookbooks as some sort of culinary soft-porn when we compare our day-to-day food experiences with the delights pictured. To paraphrase Erma Bombeck, ketchup is a valuable member of the fruits and vegetables food group. It is a staple in every Supermom's house. It borders on being *soup* in my house. Those of you without sin in this area are invited to indeed throw tomatoes. It need not omnipresent at every meal, but it can enhance the flavor of your cooking, which could probably use some enhancing now and again. Children are known to put ketchup on everything, even...well, tomatoes. And roast beef, mashed potatoes, broccoli, and yes, even the odd peanut butter sandwich. Grilled cheese sandwiches, scrambled eggs, Kraft Dinner, are all "normal" foods that require ketchup in a kid's world. It is recommended to have a "no ketchup" rule in the car (have *some* boundaries after all), while bearing in mind this may cause near mayhem every time you stop for an emergency order of fries and nuggets.

Cooking is truly a talent. Cooking a good meal in fifteen minutes or less while signing school notes, arranging frigging play dates and refereeing fights over television shows is nothing short of a miracle. In a Supermom house, a good meal is one that hasn't set off the fire alarm. Spouses are encouraged to learn the fine art of food arrangement (hide some of the black bits under the knife and fork, and the big lump of the grey stuff under the paper towel "napkin"). Supermom kids are known to ask for the "good lasagna"—the one that comes out of the freezer, not the one that you make.

Supermoms are often tempted to try out new recipes, but be warned that when you're dealing with a young family, anything other than pizza, tacos, or spaghetti is considered gross and inhumane. Children think you sit around thinking up ways to torture them by serving them food they don't like. Frankly, one of the best weapons in your child torture arsenal is to serve a meal that is nutritious and not processed.

Supermoms are not the most imaginative cooks. It's always a meat (or poultry or fish), starch (potatoes, rice, or garlic bread), and vegetable. Sometimes, when we're feeling really wild and crazy, we put out two vegetables and no starch. This is while dealing with pre-teen children who attempt to pursue a vegetarian lifestyle that makes allowances for both Big Macs and chicken nuggets.

Most Supermom kids live in fear that a new baby in the house may turn out to be allergic to peanuts in which case Supermom will have to eliminate yet another important food group in your house: peanut butter. You can't be that unlucky. Peanut butter is, for a lot of us, comfort food. Both as a reminder of our childhoods, as well as the comfort of knowing that you always have something in the house that you can put in your children's sandwiches for lunch, and they will eat it. We've all tried honey-roasted ham, cheese, liverwurst, tuna, and egg salad. None of them have the same appeal as a good old peanut butter and jelly sandwich. Tip: If these are strictly outlawed for school lunches, they'll seem like a guilty pleasure at home.

Unless you're willing to prepare the pizza and tacos they ask for every night, you're never going to satisfy your children with food they like each time. Let them be liberal with the ketchup, barbecue sauce, and mayonnaise—whatever it takes to get it down them. Underneath it all is the frozen fish stick you worked so hard to prepare especially for them. Remind yourself that eating together is what counts.

THE CHORES YOU CANNOT FINISH

When Supermoms were growing up, our mothers would often use the phrase "running the house." You know, "She's busy running the house," or "She doesn't run the house very well." What could be so difficult? When one is single and childless, it is a snap. You vacuum maybe once every two months, clean the toilets less often than that (I was never home, honestly!), and laundry could wait two weeks or so as you had smartly purchased enough underwear to take you through that length of time. This is a great Supermom-in-training strategy: Shop versus launder.

Now that we're Supermoms with children, a full time job, and probably a regular old husband, we seem to spend all of our spare time "running the house." Some Supermoms have made a wise investment and hired a regular cleaning lady (the money spent on the cleaning lady is the best money she will spend all week—even more so than the colic medicine for the baby.) You'll be doing at least two loads of laundry a day, and still the sheets on your bed are lucky to see the inside of a washing machine every two months. Towels are used until you're sure they are making you dirtier rather than drier. Daily underwear changes should be encouraged with the kids, but if they miss a day or two, it won't kill them.

And how is it that no matter how much laundry a Supermom does it's never enough? "Where are my favorite blue pants? They're the only pants I wear, you know!" "Did you wash my Pokemon shirt? All the kids are wearing them tomorrow." "Did you know it's choir pictures tomorrow? I need my black pants!" And so it goes. A smart husband should master the fine art of not verbalizing the special shirt he's looking for; rather, he should silently search for it and settle on second best if he has to.

Here then is a list of the top chores that Supermom is ultimately responsible for, and which are often started, but never finished.

1) Email. You will never be completely caught-up with your email. You may, in a wild flourish of

activity, have read each news missile, but the odds that many of them will remain unanswered is high. Take for example the "Budget Accruals End of Year Request." From last year.

2) Laundry. No sooner do you fold the last little unmatched sock than you are hit with a pile of stained, mud splattered, bloodied (and yes, you're more concerned about the shirt) pieces of clothing. You can never catch up. You earn some money—buy the little bastards (and the big one) more underwear if they insist on clean ones each time.

3) Cleaning the kitchen. From wiping the table after an overzealous pouring of cereal that morning, to sweeping the floor that night after a grievous error in judgment serving the toddler rice or spaghetti, this room will almost never be sparkling. *Please note: most men believe in the dish fairy, the bottle-washing fairy, and the fridge-stocking fairy.*

4) Linen cupboard straightening. Apparently Martha Stewart labels the shelves in her linen cupboard, e.g. bath towels, tablecloths, etc., and then neatly folds and stacks each corresponding item on its proper shelf. Supermom technique is more likely to be this: once the towels and sheets have been lucky enough to be laundered, fold them as best you can after they've been sitting in the dryer

for three days. Then open the linen cupboard, holding one arm up to stop the anticipated avalanche of badly folded linens from making their escape, and shove. Shove the towels, sheets, and other assorted linens as hard as you can into any open space in the cupboard, force the door shut (this is why you want a linen cupboard with a latching door), and then run before the wood can give way. Doors have been known to come off the hinges if not installed correctly.

5) Grocery shopping. The minute you get home from a $400 shopping trip, you run out of a necessary ingredient that has to be replaced to avoid disaster (this could be Twinkies). Bread is an impossible commodity to shop for—you either don't have enough for everyone to have toast that last morning prior to a shop, or you have too much and half of it goes moldy. What's with that?

6) Toilet paper replacement. You are the only person in the household who realizes that toilet paper is not a self-renewing resource. Anybody reading this book right now who has not shopped for, stacked, and replaced a roll of toilet paper in the last two days, this applies to you. Go and do it right now.

7) Emptying the dishwasher. An ideal Supermom kitchen would have two dishwashers and no

cupboards. One for clean dishes, one for dirty. No unstacking. End of story.

8) Bringing home the shoes under your desk. You will only ever require the shoes junked under your desk at the office, as you have no outside social life. However, you will likely attempt to fool yourself into thinking it is still a possibility and will plan each Friday afternoon to cart a few of the good ones home. Supermoms should note that rarely do shoes suitable for the office make good "going out" footwear.

9) Clothes/shoe shopping for children. Supermoms are expected to provide their children with the basics of life—shelter, food, and clothing. The clothing part is tough. They outgrow and outwear clothes faster than you can ever imagine. Kids now have to have an "indoor pair" and an "outdoor pair" of shoes for school. It's hard to keep up with one pair of sneakers that fit, let alone two. You can fortunately forget the "fancy" shoes we used to have as kids. Children are rarely dressed up anymore (birthday parties, school pictures, family holidays—surprising to see any children formally dressed for these occasions), so when the infrequent wedding or other formal gathering arises, their good shoes will never fit. Buy them black sneakers and get over it.

10) Nagging the children. Supermom kids think you love this, but no mother likes to hear herself speak when she's saying the same words over and over again. If you're nagging about chores that won't threaten their future livelihood (i.e. homework), and therefore deprive you of income in your old age, then remind them once or twice, and then punish them. For less life-impacting tasks, like cleaning their rooms, if it is not completed by an agreed-upon time, take away privileges like television, Nintendo, playing with friends, etc. Save your voice and your own sanity.

11) Stocking the right size and color pantyhose.

Time is precious, and every minute seems to count more and more when you are a Supermom. In order to keep your sanity, shift your mindset from having a "clean house," to having a house that is "clean enough." Remove anything that is growing mold, really stinky, or a health hazard. Otherwise, tidying things into small piles and taking the time found to enjoy your family, or your freedom, is well worth it. The mess will always be there. You'll have time to finish these chores when the kids leave home. And maybe, just maybe, you'll have your husband trained to do at least half of them. Dare to dream.

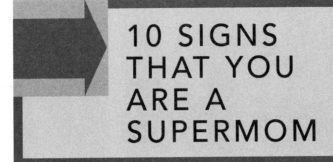

10 SIGNS THAT YOU ARE A SUPERMOM

Still unsure as to whether you fit the title of Supermom? To be clear, we're not talking about the mythical, organized, successful "bring home the bacon and cook it up in the pan" woman, but the *real* Supermom. The one who is always late for school plays, always the first to leave the office under the prying eyes of coworkers, and always the last Mom home on her block. The life of the Supermom is a role that can only be accomplished with a healthy dose of reality, humor, and a good glass of red wine. No one could possibly be as busy, harassed, and time-crunched as a Supermom.

You're not alone. Everywhere you look, Supermoms are hurrying to work, from work, and away from work in the ultimate quest of fulfilling themselves, their children, their bank balance, and occasionally even their husband's wishes (when they have time). Raise your hand if you have an unhealthy admiration of those women who didn't take their full maternity leaves, have been rumored to have two nannies in their employ, and still manage to look as if they work out on a regular basis.

The Supermom is quite easily identifiable versus the Others and the Homers. Here's a list to help you decide if you truly fall into the Supermom category.

1) You start every sentence with "I don't have time for this." This is particularly effective when speaking with coworkers regarding a marathon meeting, your boss regarding a new project, or children when being asked to fulfill obligations to do with the annual School Fun Fair.

2) You are on a first name basis with the following: dry cleaners, midnight clerk at the twenty-four-hour grocery store, internet grocery delivery person, video store clerk who accepts late charges, and the one neighborhood Homer you can call when your children are sent home sick from school. As well, you have no knowledge of the following: what your child's teacher looks like, what time school lets out for lunch, when the next "professional development" day is, and who is on the school council. (There's a school council?)

3) You have a gym membership that cost you $500 and is about to expire. This year you will

exchange the charge of $250 per visit and just buy larger clothes.

4) You offer to take the older children to the mall only when you smell a dirty diaper from the baby across the room. Advise your husband that the baby should be fine with just one last change before bedtime. Bye!

5) You know where to purchase the following at a moment's notice, day or night:

- Brownies that look homemade and can be easily transferred to one of your own plastic containers for the school bake sale, which is tomorrow.
- Plastic containers.
- Running shoes of any size, the loss of which children schedule for one day before the school sports day.
- Birthday presents for children of any age, as well as gift bags and cards. The real professionals have these stores mapped en route to the party itself.
- Flowers for your administrative assistant, wine for your coworkers, and liquor for your husband.
- "Cool" knapsacks. These are purchased versus the alternative of cleaning out the old one.

6) You have perfected the "dump and run" at your daycare. You can get in and out of the daycare prior to your baby crying, pooing, or throwing up, as well as artfully avoiding speaking to the chatty daycare employee who would like to share details about your child. You have learned to ignore the presence of the favorite blankie left on the front seat of your car as you drive away.

7) You arrange lunch dates with old friends only when you can be sure one of your children will throw up at recess.

8) You are comfortable with the decision that hats, scarves, and mittens are signs of an overprotected and coddled child. Particularly the ones who wear matching sets.

9) You are as one with frozen pizza. You have also convinced yourself that calories don't count in food that tastes like crap.

10) You consistently win the "I had a harder day than you did" competition with your husband. You are an expert at not revealing any moments of relaxation, enjoyment, or leisure in his presence.

If you recognized yourself at all, then congratulations—I think. You have truly earned the title of Supermom. Now go and get that glass of red wine. You need it.

BEWARE THE NOTES FROM SCHOOL

Nothing strikes fear into the heart of Supermom faster than a note from school. I'm not talking about the disciplinary notes that startle all parents, I'm talking about the pink, hand-drawn notes that Homers live for and Supermoms dread. "Cupcake Day" may seem innocuous enough, but at a Supermom house it's a time for prayer and retribution. Don't bother asking your children what the penalty is if they don't bring in the hallowed cakes. *Asking* the question is bad enough in their eyes—how could you possibly *not* provide them with a Tupperware container filled with cupcakes?

Supermoms are notorious for trying to get away with the donut holes in the box, which only results in the addition of an asterisk at the bottom of next month's note regarding the suitability thereof.

Supermoms try hitting the twenty-four hour supermarket on the way to school, to move the cupcakes out of their thin plastic container and into one of their own (okay, after buying a new Tupperware container because who can ever find the lid to fit the bottom?). Not good enough again. You have to bake them the night before with the children, no matter what else you have going on. They have to decorate them, so forget about doing it at midnight when the house is finally quiet. You're going to have to bite the bullet and get them done right after dinner. Accept it.

Another note you're likely to open the day it is scheduled to happen is the one for School Picture Day. Think back to your own school photos—do they make you wince or smile? I bet most people would wince. Please bear this in mind when preparing your own young for the annual photo shoot. No matter how much you primp and brush and tidy them up, they will not be happy with their photo once they're past the age of ten. Give up attempting to bribe them to wear their Sunday best for a photograph that is supposed to be a souvenir of that particular age. It is much more interesting to look back on these photos and get a sense of what they thought was a good look for them at the time. It reflects their true character.

Homers spend more time putting Little Precious together for a picture than they would on themselves over the course of a full year. Not only is a perfect result almost impossible to achieve, it puts an unfair emphasis on the importance of how you look in order to impress others. Kids don't need it at this early age; they will be submitted to this type of harsh judgment soon enough in the workforce.

Almost as frightening as School Picture Day notes are the packages for the latest fundraising activity (which seem to take place about every seven minutes in the public school system). Supermoms often end up being the only sponsor listed on their children's massive donor sheets; you are right in being loathe to take the sponsor sheets into the office and be "one of those people." And sending your children door-to-door to campaign isn't the innocent activity it used to be.

Other dreaded notes include "Please have your child bring in the following items for our annual science exhibit: two rutabagas, four rolls of toilet paper, old lightbulbs, and a shoebox." The note is always dated for the day before. As with field trip notes, parent volunteers are needed during the science fairs, pizza parties, sports days, and on and on. Once your children can read, they're very excited about your being able to participate. Get ready to disappoint them, Supermom. The dates will *always* coincide with the company's annual offsite meetings.

Solve these problems by scouring your child's mangy knapsack every night. Respond only to those messages you can, and try to get over missing out on some of them. Justify your mercenary actions by telling yourself that the Homers need these types of activities in order to remain fulfilled and be an essential part of their child's life. You'll still feel guilty, of course, for your lack of participation, but this doesn't make you a bad mother, regardless of what others who have participated may say or think. Do what you can, when you can. Good childhood memories can be made almost anywhere.

KIDS' BIRTHDAY PARTIES HAVE BECOME A COMPETITIVE SPORT

"*Supermom Hosts Best Birthday Party Ever.*" If you've ever imagined this headline, you really are working too hard. In the past, rousing games of musical chairs, "egg and spoon" races, and potato sack races were not only mandatory, but, in fact, all that was required. Another favorite of this Supermom involved shelled peanuts hung from the basement ceiling with string, which one had to jump up and bite off.

How times have changed. There's no way you could have a birthday party with a peanut, or any

nut, anywhere in the vicinity, given the prepon-
derance of peanut allergies these days (what's that
about, anyway?). Supermom must know the "in"
character for the main theme, as all childhood
activities today have to be branded. You need Spiderman blindfolds, Pokemon paper plates, and
SpongeBob SquarePants wrapping paper. Gone are
the days when the goody bags (or "loot bags" as
they are more aptly called today) were plain brown
paper and contained maybe a pencil, a ruler, and
one chocolate bar.

Well, Supermoms, it's a whole new world. Today
we have to compete on venue, number of attendees (more children shows affluence, apparently),
food, loot bags, and presents. The venues run the
gamut from indoor playgrounds to bowling alleys,
movie theatres, rock climbing gyms, swimming
pools, indoor beach volleyball...the list expands
every year. These are expensive options, and once
the food is added on you're looking at a small
mortgage to pay it off. There are birthday parties
for three-year-olds that include an adult buffet of
high quality food found in the best restaurants.
Even the breadsticks and pizza should be ordered
from a small gourmet shop.

The loot bags seem to have escalated in value,
and are now mostly seen to offset the cost of the

gift. Your kids will come home with watches, expensive hair accessories, and expensive trading cards. The children are fully aware of the value of these bags, and they'll readily compare them with other loot bags from other parties. If you think you can get away without offering up a loot bag due to the cost of the venue, think again.

Make sure you plan something your children will enjoy, but tell them that they can't have more kids than they are years old (i.e. a seven-year-old with seven guests), and that number will be halved if it's a sleepover. Certain venues (i.e. hotel rooms) are simply too much. Be creative and have a retro birthday party with all the "egg and spoon" races and hokey games we had in our childhood. You'll be pleasantly surprised how much the kids enjoy themselves. Try to stem the competitiveness in your children's' circle. And save yourself from having to make embarrassing calls to "Coco the Clown" in the middle of your next management update meeting.

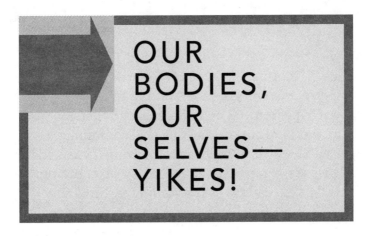

OUR BODIES, OUR SELVES— YIKES!

One of the biggest adjustments you'll have to make as a Supermom is your new Superbod. Supersized, that is. Having a baby is an incredible experience. Too bad your body doesn't feel the same way. Supermoms by definition have a post-pregnancy body (yes, five years is still post). There is flab where you didn't know flab could exist (what's with back fat, for instance?), things sag that you didn't know were saggable, and everything is just...well, softer. At the beginning, you take some pleasure that your body has been a wonderful vessel for life; later on, you just want the old body back. And to fit into your snappy little business suits.

After the birth of any child, with another birthday of your own approaching, and the push to get back to normal before you return to the office, Supermoms will be super-determined to get back into shape. You will be so determined that you may start working out the day the local community center will take your baby for babysitting (at less than six weeks). Start with the exercise bike, but don't overdo it. Pedaling for forty minutes, three times a week is not a good exercise plan for someone who, with a recent childbirth experience, has likely grown a hemorrhoid. You will suffer through the next two weeks afraid to sit down. This pain will be worse than the episiotomy stitches.

The best advice for Supermom is to slow down and try to eat sensibly, which is not easy if you have a house full of children, especially when your older children beg you to share their unhealthy snacks. Try instead to go back to the gym when the baby is at least six months old. It feels good to reclaim your body. As you look around the gym, you will be heartened to see all kinds of women getting fit and taking time for themselves. You'll feel like you're a part of something.

All of these wondrous bodies are also on display in the locker room. We really do come in all shapes and sizes. Are women getting better at accepting themselves for what they look like? Can we stop torturing ourselves to look like supermodels? Supermoms have a hard time letting this ideal go.

Two old friends meet up, and their conversation goes like this.

"Wow, Helen, you look great. Look at you—you've lost so much weight. I haven't seen you here lately, where have you been working out?"

"Actually, I've been sick and not able to eat very much, so that accounts for most of this."

"What did you have?"

"West Nile Virus. It was horrible. I couldn't eat, couldn't sleep, I had massive headaches, and was very tired."

Silence for a moment.

"And now you're so thin!"

"I know. Isn't it great?"

Just hope that you don't run into any of your neighbors in the locker room. There's something wrong about seeing casual acquaintances in the nude. Total strangers, fine. Close friends, fine also. But people you only pass on the sidewalk every few weeks...well, you don't want to know whether they have a Brazilian bikini wax or not. You will desperately hope they don't discuss the state of your body and associated body hair with other neighbors they come across.

"Do you know her, in the house on the corner? Wicked cellulite, overgrown armpits, and wouldn't know a matching bra and panty set if it hit her in the face."

Is it possible to have grown fat that is completely resilient to removal? It seems that you can work away at the same twenty pounds that has dogged you for the past ten years. Every once in a while you might get a rush of fat loss on the scales—say two or three pounds—but then the next time you gleefully hop on (with natural grace and style) it's back, and it's brought some fatty friends too.

So there you are, Supermom, madly pedaling away at the exercise bike, on your way to nowhere, and the only thing that keeps you going is the thought that you're streamlining your thighs into taut, lithe limbs with each turn of the wheel. That and the fact that for a blissful hour you have traded your two children away to the crowded and optimistically titled "Play Center" downstairs. You will have to walk past the closed door of the Play Center between the ladies' locker room and the exercise studio, and if you try really hard, you can block out the sounds of my children crying as you scurry past.

Supermoms are dismayed to find out that they have run out of excuses not to get back into shape. The childbearing years may be over, the clothes no longer fit, and you are only two scant sizes away from having to trade up to the "big and fat" shops. It's time. You can try to convince yourself that your favorite clothing store has resized all of its clothes, which would explain your ascension up their size rankings.

Walking through the change room, Supermom avoids looking at herself in the mirror. That thing you see hanging down the back of your leg is not a loose thread from your decrepit white cotton underwear, but a piece of your ass that has finally given up its fight with gravity and is aiming straight for the floor.

Just because Supermoms think about their weight every single day, at least once, they may feel that they are obsessed with their weight. They are not. Find me a woman, Supermom, Homer, or Other, who doesn't. Either in a good way or a bad way, it's part of our lifestyle, the way masturbation is for men. They think about their penises all the time; we devote our brains to thinner thighs in thirty days.

Once you're showered and fully dressed, you might contemplate the option of walking right past the Play Center and stopping for a quiet coffee, or worse, leaving the premises altogether. Someone would notice if two children were left behind at the end of the day. You'd notice too; you might miraculously get everything *done* you set out to do with your precious spare time. Children have radar to determine the worst time to interrupt whatever activity you're engaging in. From going to the washroom, to finally getting around to hemming up your children's pants, which probably don't even need hemming anymore. They choose these times to shout "Mom, you need to come here. I didn't *mean* to." Grudgingly, you head to the Play Center.

You retrieve the bawling infant from the now stationary swing as the toddler disentangles herself from a group of rabid-looking children. Don't ask if they had fun, because frankly you don't want to know if they didn't. You need this time to reflect upon your fat and to string together more than two thoughts without the constant interruptions from the children.

A healthy Supermom is a happy Supermom. Nothing thrills us more than the ability to button up some pre-pregnancy pants and look in the mirror without sucking our cheeks in (both sets). This good mood could absorb juice spills, sibling fights, late husbands, and even the occasional muscle strain. Exercise your body and you'll find your mind is healthier, too.

PART 2:

Like Saturday
Night Fever, It
Starts Out
Sexy But Ends
with Really
Bad Clothing
and Some
Uncomfortable
Positions

"If pregnancy were a book, they would cut the last two chapters."

—Nora Ephron

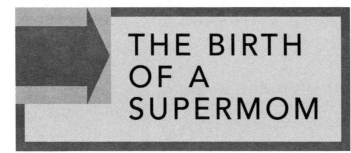

THE BIRTH OF A SUPERMOM

Remember that scene from *Alien?*

Come on, you know which scene I mean. Where the little green toothy fella pops right out of that guy's stomach in the middle of mealtime. Oh, yeah. That's the one. You thought your Senior Vice President was scary—hang on. Welcome to the wonderful world of pregnancy, birth (see reference to scene above), and coping with the seemingly unreasonable demands of a newborn baby. The screaming, the crying, the sleepless nights...but enough about the husbands. When you enter the world of the Supermom, it's a nightmare, right from the start.

Supermoms go through the pregnancy mill and experience the pain and trauma that all women do, and that includes conception. No matter how good or bad the "performance" was that evening, that truly was the *fun* part of this deal. The rest of the experience may be rewarding, fulfilling, yada, yada, yada, but "fun" is not a word you will hear very often when describing any pregnancy.

Your body will go through changes you cannot be prepared for. Have you heard about the shoe size thing? The tear duct challenge? The line down your stomach? The vaginal dryness? Ouch. Okay, I didn't need to mention that last one, especially if you're in the last stages of pregnancy and even a tampon won't be welcome *for the rest of your life*. Well, buckle up, gals. It's going to be a bumpy ride, or rather a ride that produced a bump, in this case. Oh, and just a reminder, Supermom—while you're going through all of this, you still have to attend that three-day off-site in Des Moines, and get the monthly activity reports in on time.

Companies that manufacture early pregnancy tests know what they're doing. Their design makes it impossible not to pee on your own fingertips. If this grosses you out to the point of nausea, then you're clearly not ready for motherhood. You'll come to embrace the notion of *only* getting hit with urine, which is, we are led to believe, sterile. This will also begin your training for the urine sample Olympics, which you will be entering as a full competitor once your pregnancy is confirmed.

So you've washed your hands (three times, with

disinfectant soap), and you're waiting to see if the thin blue line will confirm your worst fears, one way or the other. Congratulations, you're pregnant. Now what? Shouldn't you feel different, act different, *be* different? You are. You have joined the world of "those who have no life." And I couldn't be happier for you. All of the things you thought were important yesterday are not so pressing today...until your boss is on the line. You are growing a human life, and for that you should be rewarded. (Your children can be entering their teen years and there's still no visible sign of a reward, but that's another story.) If being a parent teaches you anything, it's faith. Faith that you'll get through another day with the little rats, and faith that any "bad Mommy" moments you'll undoubtedly experience will not be captured forever on video.

So you did it. You peed on the stick and the lines turned blue. For those of you who are not pregnant for the first time, you knew this before the home pregnancy test. You knew it because: a) your boobs have been killing you, b) you haven't had to restock your tampons, c) you had just finally lost all the weight from the last baby, or d) you just got promoted. The moment you discover you're pregnant, many, many thoughts and questions immediately race through your head. Boy? Girl? Twins? Due date? Weight gain? Big boobs from breastfeeding? Work? Body? His? Then the next ten seconds will be full of doubts about your ability to do this, your husband's ability to do this, and your baby's ability to survive despite the two or seven cocktails you had last week, which was, of course, in celebration of finally getting down to your dream weight and/or your promotion.

Relax, the baby is probably fine. It's you that you have to look out for from now on. As you venture out into the real world, secure with the knowledge that a little human being is softly nestled within you, you'll find it hard to believe that anything else in your life will ever be as important. That's great. That's the right feeling to have. It's the right thing to be thinking during the long-term strategy planning sessions at work, and during the five-minute wait through the drive-thru at the coffee shop. Being pregnant is an intrinsically great feeling, but there are some words of advice I feel it is my duty to pass on to you, the new Supermom-To-Be.

* Contrary to your beliefs, you are not the first woman to experience the following while pregnant: morning sickness, a husband who just doesn't understand, and the most inter-fering mother-in-law in the world.

* During the course of your pregnancy, many people will attempt to predict the sex of your child based on the size of your stomach, the *way* you carry the baby (I only ever noticed one way—in front), the sheen in your hair, your complexion, the fullness of your face, or even with a needle, a thread, and your open palm. Let me tell you this: monkeys would have the same odds as these freaks.

* You'll be certain you've made the wrong decision as to whether or not to go back to work after the birth of your child. You'll make the right one, by the way.

* Ninety-nine percent of women do not look better when they're pregnant (Kate Moss excepted). However, you will look pregnant, not fat, and you will have license to eat, so enjoy yourself. Who are you trying to attract anyway? You're already knocked up, and the concept of sex for pleasure is foreign to you. This holds true for five years after the birth of the child as well.

* Maternity clothes are designed by skinny, cigarette-smoking, sexy, twenty-two-year-olds who want you to look old and fat. You don't need the extra help, frankly. Choose a similar style of clothing to what you wore

before you were pregnant. If you wore button-down shirts and khakis before, don't try to do black tights and miniskirts.

* Your boobs will get bigger, but no one will notice except you and your husband. Your stomach makes all things relative.

* Your baby is growing inside your stomach, but your ass will get bigger as well.

* You will gain weight not only in all the obvious places, but in your ankles, your feet (both length and width), and that space between your underarm and the side of your bra.

* Strange people (not just strangers, but strange people) will rub your stomach. Wouldn't it be great if just once someone would rub the father's penis and say, "How wonderful for you"? This would be the most action the father has had since conception, so everyone wins.

* Hardly anyone wants to know the details of your last ultrasound/vaginal examination/urine color or baby heart rate, except maybe your husband and other pregnant women.

Doesn't sound pretty, does it? It's not fair that pregnancy happens to the sex who cares most about their body image, but perhaps the two go hand-in-hand. To repeat, pregnancy is a license to eat without guilt, and every woman should have that at least once in her life after the age of ten.

YOU, A SUPERMOM?

So the time has come to announce to your friends, coworkers, and members outside your immediate family of your upcoming big event. In North America, this normally comes at the three-month (or in pregnant woman terms, the twelfth week) mark, when it is generally agreed that the biggest risk of miscarriage has passed. In many ways, announcing your pregnancy is thrilling, but none more so than letting everyone know that your little belly is not due to overeating.

Prepare to get mixed reactions on the announcement of your pregnancy. They may include:

* Her, a mother? *Okaaaaayyyy...*
* Her, a mother? She's always had the hips for it.
* Hope it's his. On the other hand, he's no Tom Cruise.

* She has no idea what she's in for. Lucky her.
* She has no idea what she's in for. I'll tell her.
* Oh, goody. Another reason to break out my own childbirth story. Can't forget about using the phrase "from stem to stern."
* Darn, I thought she was just getting fat.
* Lost that $5 in the office pool.
* I thought they said they're supposed to glow. Okay, if acne counts.
* Ewww. Just pictured her and her hubby doing it.

And that's just from your immediate family. At work, it's a whole other story. Women who have just come back from maternity leaves will look at you with envy and longing. Men will say, "That's great. Now are you in this next meeting or what?" and totally forget about your status until the day your water breaks in their office. Your boss will say, "When are you due?" while mentally reworking your entire position, the department, and thinking it'll be a long time before they hire another childbearing-aged woman into their group.

Some Supermoms can be lucky enough to accrue vacation weeks even while on maternity leave, which prompts many Other bosses to ask: "Why do women on maternity leave need vacation time when they come back? Isn't it one big vacation anyway?" While part of Supermom is secretly looking forward to a break from the routine of work, and that aspect alone would qualify as a vacation of sorts, part of you should want to forcibly confine these Others to your house for a week when the baby arrives. Real Supermoms are not supposed to look forward to their maternity leaves, rather they are to expedite them.

Your pregnancy announcement may have another interesting side effect. Pregnancies seem to come in waves in many offices. All of a sudden you will notice there are a flock of tubby gals walking about. Perhaps it's because pregnancy serves as a wake-up call to those around us who haven't yet taken the plunge. Or taken it again, in some cases. When a woman ten years younger than yourself is stating that "it's now or never" or "I don't want to be fifty before they start school," then it hits home.

Throughout your pregnancy in the workplace, you will experience both the good and the bad. The bad is the ill-fitting clothes that replace your sleek career wear, the desperately ravenous moments in the "mother" of four-hour-long meetings, the achy boobs, and the sore back. The good is the unexpected kick you get from within during a marathon planning session, and the wonderful moments of daydreaming when the forward planning process involves the weeks when you'll be on maternity leave. The good is also the morning after the rest of the team has been out celebrating a recent success with copious amounts of alcohol, and you're the one with the clear head, for a change. Then again, clear heads aren't all that common in pregnant women.

I'm sure you've been warned about the "Pregnancy Brain" phenomena. It's normally a general state of fuzziness, bad memory, losing sentences, losing thoughts, and generally being a little bit ditzy most of the time. If you're blonde not too many people will notice the difference. Oh, you're not really blonde, come on. Anyway, the pregnant brain doesn't seem to be able to function quite as efficiently as the pre-pregnant brain because there is so much more stuff crowding our limited grey matter.

So what's on the mind of a pregnant woman? Many otherwise mundane situations and experiences suddenly take on much bigger significance. The nose that suits your husband but nonetheless frightens you if you catch it at the wrong angle could turn up on your baby. Or, the dumpy butt you've been dragging around your whole life, which no amount of squats will reduce, will not only get bigger on you but could turn up on an adorable four-year-old girl. What about family? Will I see more of the in-laws? Less? Are my parents really happy about becoming grandparents? What about work? Will I lose opportunities because I'm pregnant? Why won't they cut me some slack?

Many other random thoughts will occur to you during the normal workday. Will my baby be as rotten as that kid next door? Is the baby supposed to sleep on its back, front, or side? Is there a baby rotisserie on the market, to cover all angles? How come they don't make "girl" diapers and "boy" diapers anymore? There is a difference, you know. How many diapers are in the landfills already? What if they outlaw disposable diapers and I have to use cloth like some tree-hugging freak? Does breastfeeding really suck all the shape out of your boobs and leave them like two deflated balloons stuck to a plank? What if I don't know what cool baby clothes are? What if the name we give our baby turns out to be the first name of the biggest mass murderer of all time? What if our child hates his/her name and changes it to Bambi? Am I pregnant enough to wear maternity clothes? Why can't I just wear my normal clothes with a big safety pin at the back? Who looks back there? Have you looked back there? Don't look back there! Stretch marks fade, right? Okay, they're sexy, right?

With all of these questions and competing thoughts, it's no wonder our minds drift off into La La Land once in a while. Wait until you see how your brain operates on only two hours sleep. These days will seem lucid.

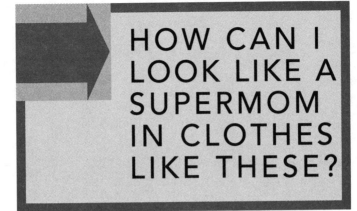

HOW CAN I LOOK LIKE A SUPERMOM IN CLOTHES LIKE THESE?

Supermoms-In-Training will face many new challenges in the workplace during their pregnancies. One of the biggest will be a shrunken work wardrobe: you'll go from ten to twenty fashionable outfits to one or two maternity outfits. The one or two that still make you look professional and attractive.

Don't believe that black is slimming when you're pregnant. If you ever hear these words from a maternity clothing store employee, walk out, never to return. Clearly there will be no words of truth ever uttered by this staff. You are pregnant. Get over yourself. You will not look slim for the next six months or so, so buy clothes that will flatter you, not attempt to disguise your blimp-like figure.

Mood swings? Never more so than in a bunch of hormone-crazed women trying on maternity clothes: "Yay, I'm pregnant" to "Boo hoo, I'm so fat."

You might have been told that you can avoid some of the high cost of maternity clothes by buying at the larger size stores. I did not find this to be true.

Repeat after me: there are no hip or chic or "business-like" maternity clothes. This is also not the time to discover a new image, new designer, or try out previously unflattering colors. You're just yourself, after all, only bigger in places. Please avoid the following maternity disasters:

* Any shirt which indicates in one way or another there is a "baby under construction." This is almost as sickening as those "baby on board" signs which frequent the overzealous first-time parents' minivans.

* The infamous "Peter Pan" collar. If you don't know what this is, then you deserve to be plagued by doubt each time you purchase a new blouse.

* Any pants referred to as "slacks," unless you are that rare sixty-five-year-old grandmother who decided to get pregnant.

* Stripes. Can cause double vision in innocent bystanders.

* Tight shoes. Most pregnant women's ankles turn into fat little sausages. Stuffing them into too tight, too fashionable shoes only draws attention to them. Can cause sharp intakes of breath in witnesses.
* Your husband's clothes. Unless you would normally wear them if they had shrunk in the wash. He'll resent you wearing them, and they won't look great on you right now.

Some maternity clothing stores are helpful enough to provide you with a fake bump or pillow to strap around your stomach to see how the clothes will fit in your eighth and ninth month. This is necessary only if you aren't showing yet. Otherwise, do not use the pillow. Any clothes bought in month three or four you will not want to wear in month eight or nine. Plus, unless they have other pillows to strap to your ass, thighs, and boobs, you won't be getting anywhere close to the true picture anyhow.

Maternity clothing manufacturers try in vain to keep up with current fashion, even on the underwear front. Most Supermoms know that only underwear you can fold four times is real maternity underwear, so why mess with success? Apparently Supermoms are now expected to embrace thong underwear. Most Supermoms try it at least once. While others may rave about the thrill, most will find it is just as depraved and disgusting as they feared. It isn't comfortable, and no matter how toned and sexy you think you are (even while pregnant), they just seem to go where they shouldn't be going.

Some of the cooler, sexier Supermoms admit to buying them and "getting used to them," but with children a Supermom's wardrobe will be more built around comfort than style (just ask my twelve-year-old).

It wasn't until the ads for thong pantyliners appeared that Supermoms got really worried. They had clearly gone mainstream. Know also that this is one item of clothing that, once purchased, will never be accepted for a return. With a nervous gait many Supermoms may set out for the mall to find the perfect pair. You'll feel a bit naughty (or maybe cheeky), and a bit scared of what you might find.

There are many, many racks of thongs available. Keep trying to picture a sleek smooth backside in your favorite black work pants, instead of the elasticized tummy slacks you're now wearing.

So here's the thing. They *are* as uncomfortable as you might think. You have spent years trying to keep your underwear out of the very place these are designed to sit. Comfortable? No. Sexy? You're kidding, right? When you're pregnant? Literally, please don't even go there. Sensible Supermoms decide that this may well be the one trend that will have to pass them by.

BACK UP THE TRUCK AND GET OUT OF THE WAY

There are still some pre-Supermom women who believe that their lives will remain relatively unchanged once the baby arrives. They might even believe their homes and wallet will remain unscathed by the simple inclusion of a tiny little baby. Ha! From play saucers to breezy swinging action, you'll want to take advantage of every piece of furniture that can help you in your sacred quest with baby in the first year: getting them to shut up and go to sleep. Nothing is as quiet as the sound of a newborn baby sleeping. There are many baby accessories available for parents in the new millennium, so pay attention.

The *crib* is obviously the most indispensable piece of furniture for a newborn baby. It is not a coincidence that it closely resembles a cage. With your first born, you'll worry that within the first week baby will be able to somehow use the bumper pads, mobile, and puffy quilt as tools to vault headfirst onto the floor below. You'll be frantic about baby's comfort, placing twenty or so stuffed animals in a specific order every night and naptime. The baby cannot see these animals. They're unable to focus in the first weeks, plus you'll likely lay them at their feet to avoid suffocating. Tip: lose the animals.

The *bumper pads* in a crib function to stop baby from bashing his head into the rails...I think. They may be purely decorative, but they only maintain that nice straight edge for about a week and half, and then they resemble an irregularly stuffed, strangely flat pillow. They do not wash well, but if your baby happens to be that one in a million who doesn't get some bodily fluid on some part of the pads, then you're in luck.

The *mobile* is another strange invention. Who likes the music on these things? The baby? He can't hear it above his own screaming. Four-year-old siblings may like the tune on the baby's mobile, but who cares? You don't want *them* in the baby's room making noise. And besides, the music will do nothing to offset the pain each time you bash baby's head against it when you blearily pull him out of the crib in the middle of the night. Again, decorative only until the aforementioned four-year-old climbs into the crib and pulls off the four stuffed teddy bears for her own personal collection.

Have you ever changed a crib sheet? It's tighter than a Chief Financial Officer in the last quarter budget session. It is akin to wrestling a pair of Celine Dion's jeans onto Kirstie Alley's butt. I'm not sure why the manufacturers produce their crib sheets one size too small for all standard crib mattresses, but you'll find that the only way to change these suckers is to remove the mattress from the crib and wrestle it onto the ground. It's somewhat like changing the diaper of a squirming baby. By the way, you can only get the mattress out of the crib once you've dismantled the mobile, untied the bumper pads, and removed all twenty stuffed animals...yet another reason to think twice about adding these accoutrements.

Ah, the *baby swing*. Say it with me now, sisters: *We love the swing. We love the swing.* Why? The baby loves the swing. Now some parents tell me not all babies love the swing, and I'm glad I've never met one of these foreign creatures. Your first baby will go in the swing at three months. Your second at two months. The third at two weeks. The fourth...well, at least the hospital bracelets should be off. The swing only lasts for about six months, sadly, at which point the little bastards can grab the side rails and they become an unsafe and unwise choice. Enjoy it while you can.

The *ExerSaucer* is the mutant offspring of that long ago loved favorite, the walker (on wheels). The original walkers were banned in some countries years ago because of the number of accidents involving stairs. They haven't outlawed ride-on cars or trucks, which are even more dangerous, but there you go. The ExerSaucer is a great invention that allows Junior to be propped up in a safe place to play with whatever toys are attached to the accompanying tray. Make sure to heed the safety directions on your ExerSaucer, which include reasonable warnings not to use it as a flotation device, drag it behind a car, or (gasp) attach wheels to it. These have a limited life; once baby can crawl, the restriction is not welcome.

The best advice you'll receive is to buy the *playpen* months before you require it, i.e. before the baby is independently mobile. They get used to it as a place to be, versus a place to stop them from where they're going. They're great for overnight trips. The best uses are to block doorways, as a Christmas tree holder (baby can't reach ornaments), and a toy bin.

The *Bouncing Bounceroo,* also known as a Johnny JumpUp or, as it's known in many homes, the "Jump and Dump." Babies have an uncanny propensity to "let loose" (their bowels, that is) while jumping gleefully from these bouncy door frame attachments. These are also great fun; however, watch out for the eight-year-old boy studying medieval catapults at school.

The *high chair* is another way to stop Junior from getting around and grabbing your dinner, but mostly is a place for baby to store wet, mushy strawberries under his behind, while wearing his new pale blue Easter outfit. Don't look into the crevices of the vinyl seat too closely.

There are many other mechanisms on the market that can house and store your baby. They're all different, and not everything works with every child. Just remember, money can't buy happiness, but it can buy ten minutes of peace and quiet.

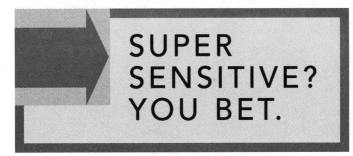

SUPER SENSITIVE? YOU BET.

Men (spouses and coworkers alike) are notorious for saying and doing the wrong thing at the wrong time; during your pregnancy is no exception. On the next few pages are a few words of wisdom to pass on to them. Leave this book open in the bathroom at home, or sneak it in an office toilet stall, where they regularly look for reading material. Men should notice that there are only a few stock answers/comments that are acceptable. Memorize them.

What Men Say:	What Men Should Say:
Man, you're huge!	You look great. Can't even tell you're pregnant.
Is it normal to gain that much weight?	You look great. Can't even tell you're pregnant.
Wow, did the boob fairy visit? I love your new big boobs.	Are they bigger? I think they're just perfect no matter what.
You mean you gain weight in your thighs, too?	Are they bigger? I think they're just perfect no matter what.
Your whole face has changed. I didn't know it would affect your face.	You look great. Can't even tell you're pregnant.

What Men Say:	What Men Should Say:
I've never seen you eat so much. Do you have to eat that much?	I'm not the one who's eating for two. You enjoy it.
How much are our grocery bills now?	I'm not the one who's eating for two. You enjoy it.
The doctor said it was okay to have sex. It won't hurt the baby.	You must be exhausted. Let me know if I can get you anything on my way to the shower.
Just because we can't have intercourse doesn't mean you can't make *me* happy.	You must be exhausted. Let me know if I can get you anything on my way to the shower.
Come on, after the baby is born we'll be too tired for this.	You look great. Can't even tell you're pregnant.

What Men Say:	What Men Should Say:
Are you sure you're not carrying twins? Jane in my office never got this big. You know Jane, the cute one.	You look great. Can't even tell you're pregnant.
I read somewhere that women only need to gain ten to fifteen pounds during pregnancy. The rest is just fat.	You look great. Can't even tell you're pregnant.
You've changed since our wedding day.	You look great. Can't even tell you're pregnant.

By now, men, you should get the idea. Pregnant women know precisely how big they are, how much weight they've gained, and how they used to look. You don't need to remind them. Just dance around the subject and ignore that big white elephant in the room...that's an expression, not a comment on her figure.

THE COUNTDOWN HAS BEGUN

Now that some time has passed and you've experienced some bodily trauma already, the countdown to labor and delivery will begin. Unlike the Leadership Training Course at work, this torturous process cannot be continually rescheduled. The minute you find out you're pregnant, particularly for the first time, you start counting down the months, weeks, days, and sometimes in a moment of blind panic, the hours until *that* day will come. Like women who look forward more to the wedding than the marriage, many women dread childbirth more than having a child. This is wrong. Childbirth is not pleasant; it's downright horrifying, but it doesn't last a lifetime. Raising a child does.

The countdown to the due date or delivery week is constantly running through a pregnant woman's mind. Every date, time, and event will be judged on its proximity to the time when you're going to somehow expel this giant growth into the outside world, using only your own tiny orifice. It is scary. The constant reminders that "millions of women do it every day" will do nothing to calm or placate the pregnant woman. There will be many nights when you will look over at your husband and silently (or at the top of your lungs) curse him for not being the one who will have to go through with this. This is one of the rare things in life where there truly is no turning back.

Do not wish this time away. This is precious, quiet, sleep-filled time that you will never get back once the child is born. Take advantage of every pedicure special, every movie, every play and cultural event as your wallet and bladder will allow. Read. Sit. Eat. It'll be here soon enough. Work hard at the office—this is the *least* tired you will be for a long time…really.

To prepare for delivery, you will undoubtedly get either talked into or be inspired to take prenatal classes. Your husband will not want to attend, no matter what he says. He *will* attend, no matter what he says. Many of these classes take place at hospitals, which is comforting, but also drives home the point that this is indeed a "big deal." With doctors and nurses and everything.

The classes include many comforting, and many horrifying, pieces of information. First of all, yes, as you had suspected, that's where the baby will come out. And secondly, yes, it does seem as though pushing a watermelon through a drinking straw would be more reasonable. Even the men will flinch when they hear words like "episiotomy" and "slight tearing." What is "slight tearing" anyway? Either you tear, or you don't, and the thought conjures images of Hannibal Lecter. They will demonstrate how the baby will edge its way down the birth canal (sounds lovely, but isn't), and the various stages of labor. Here's a realistic interpretation of the three stages:

Stage 1) It hurts. More than your worst menstrual pain. About a jillion times worse.

Stage 2) It really hurts. Where are the drugs?

Stage 3) Thank goodness for the drugs. Where are my magazines?

The good news is, it doesn't go on forever. The bad news is, it lasts way longer than conception, especially Stage Two (the really hurting part). You'll get the usual lecture on "natural birth" versus "medically assisted" births. If you're not turned on by a "natural appendectomy," I don't think you'll be excited about a "natural birth" either.

Another class session will likely cover your Birth Plan. What the hell? You plan on having a birth, you think sensibly. Don't plan on thinking about it too much. These things can be overanalyzed. Again, it hurts, you take drugs, and then it doesn't hurt. Simple. But oh no, they want you to think about what it's going to be like, from beginning to end. It's like Catholic priests trying to advise couples on marriage. You have no idea what you're in for, and you'll feel like an idiot once you've done it and it's nothing like you thought. You'll wax on about the breathing techniques, go on about the massages your partner will give you. You'll fantasize about the pureness and the beauty of the moment, the realization of true love, and the fulfillment of all your womanly expectations.

Yeah, right. You'll be breathing only to break up the screaming and moaning, telling your husband to get out of your face when he attempts to come within three feet of you, then shrieking at him to come closer to hold the hair out of your face while you throw up into a bed pan, and then vowing never to allow any foreign objects larger than a tampon to enter your body ever again. Birth plan, my foot. Try planning your next traffic accident—you'll have more luck seeing it through.

MAN, I USED TO BE SO COOL!

All Supermoms at one time or another have asked themselves: "How did I get here? What happened? Two minutes ago I was a young, single, somewhat slim, happening gal out on the town, staying up until 2:00 in the morning, throwing up, suffering a hangover..." then as the thought progresses, the reality sets in. As a Supermom, you're still up at 2:00 a.m. and there is barf involved—it's just not yours anymore.

Getting pregnant is a sexy thing. At the beginning. Having sex for the purpose of producing a baby is very cool, if you're lucky and get knocked up right away. If you find yourself consulting calendars, thermometers, and fertility doctors, the pleasure is somewhat diluted. Nothing can prepare you for the thrill of finding out that you're carrying a baby. It's so thrilling that a lot of us react by running to the toilet to throw up. This is nature's way of giving you practice in the fine art of cleaning up bodily functions, which becomes one of your primary roles as a parent. The fatigue is no accident either.

Pregnancy can be a great time if your health is good and you're generally feeling well. It's basically a license to eat. After years and years of dieting and counting calories, you now have an excuse and you should take advantage of it. I'm not talking about eating to excess and being the "bad example" on a daytime talk show. Just being able to have real cheese instead of low fat, that extra slice of pizza, and the occasional chocolate bar is nirvana for some of us. Believe me, it's going to be tough to take off the weight afterwards, but you may as well enjoy it while you can.

When Supermom was a cool girl out on the town, she probably liked to think her fashion sense was pretty good too. Not haute couture or cutting edge, but it at least addressed the current trends and made the most of an average body. During pregnancy you are expected to ignore any self-esteem your wardrobe might have contributed to, and venture into the world of stores with names like "Thyme Maternity Wear" (*"Thyme to get some ugly clothes"*) and "From Here to Maternity" (*From where? Planet Ugly?*). Then there's the maternity clothing with the label T.W.B. I'm not sure what it stands for, but once someone suggested it was "The Wide Butt," that definition stuck with me.

Maternity fashions leave something to be desired, to put it mildly. They are designed either to accentuate the belly, or detract from it, neither of which works. Pick a few basic pieces and stick with them, because no matter what you do, you're never going to look like Sarah Jessica Parker did when she was pregnant—all belly, tight ass, and long, thin legs. Doesn't happen. And even though your pregnancy will seem like nine years instead of nine months (it's ten; the men must have done the math on that one), it will, in retrospect, be over in a flash, so enjoy it. Please, don't talk yourself into thinking it's sensible to wear those maternity clothes a month or two after you've given birth. Yes, people can tell they're maternity clothes, and yes, people are tired of seeing you in them—people meaning mostly you.

The first few weeks of motherhood are like nothing you've experienced before. You're tired and cranky, the house is messy, your spouse is shell-shocked, the baby is frantic, etc., etc. This too shall pass. Take whatever help is offered, and when you're snapping at your husband or family members, remember it's not their fault you're so tired. It's just part of what you have to go through to get to the end. Helpful people may tell you the first four to six weeks are the worst. You will count the days. At precisely six weeks and one day, you will feel totally ripped off that your baby is still crying and you still feel "the worst." (When that child is twelve years old you would honestly give anything to have five minutes with her as an infant again.)

The idea of having a baby is like a nice warm woolen blanket you pull around yourself, only to discover the wool is sort of itchy, there's a small hole in the bottom corner, and the color only slightly suits you. But all in all, it's still warm and you wouldn't trade it away for anything. I don't think everyone should have children. Besides the jokes about how two aesthetically challenged people (a.k.a. *butt ugly*) shouldn't go this route, I think it goes beyond that.

People who say they're "too selfish" to have children probably are (meet the Others). And there's nothing wrong with that. It's better than parents who regret having children and avoid them through working long hours or taking adult-only holidays.

Not all moments with children are golden—far from it. You would still do it all over again. You can forgo being cool—not just while you're pregnant, but forever. Once you're someone's mother, you can never be cool again. Lisa Marie Presley was being interviewed and she said that she would have to "drag her children along," because they didn't want to hang out with their mother. If Lisa Marie can't get her children to believe *she's* cool, believe me, you can't.

Having a baby also means that you are now the grown-up. With many Supermoms waiting to have children until the career is on track, it can be a bit of a shock to discover that not only do you have to grow up, you're already old.

When our parents were 40, they were old. When you hit this ominous milestone, you can't help but feel that you're no longer...well, young. Supermoms, it's a tough transition from being the youngest at the office to realizing that most of your staff are young enough to be your children.

What are the true characteristics of being old? Even Supermoms grow old. You might see yourself here:

1) You buy shoes mostly for comfort, instead of for style. This does not include the toe-pinching high heels that you wear twice a year for office Christmas parties and (second) weddings. This means day-to-day comfort.

2) The number one reason you like your haircut is because "it's easy." This may be because after all these years you've finally found a style that doesn't take you forty minutes, three hot electrical appliances, and multiple "product" applications just to open the front door for a newspaper.

3) Your favorite restaurant is convenient. This is opposed to the more trendy eateries, which require research, investigation, advance reservations, and knowledge of the backstreets of the city.

4) You buy white t-shirts from Wal-Mart because they're cheap, and because you have children, you're always there. You save the $40.00 Gap t-shirts for special occasions, when you wrest them out of your pre-teen daughter's hands.

5) You make dinners that hit all the major food groups—even going so far as to prepare dishes that you yourself don't even like. Gone are the days of popcorn and diet coke for a main meal.

6) You slip on ice and feel the aftereffects for at least a week. And you don't mind telling people it's because "we're all getting older." A good line as it drags everyone around you down to your level of decrepidness.

7) You scan the obituaries for classmates, instead of your parents' friends. You also scan the birth announcements in order not to miss out on friends'

successful fertility treatments that you haven't heard about because you have no social life anymore.

The bad news is you're not cool once you have children. The good news is you don't have the time to give a shit.

PART 3:

A Very Brief
and Highly
Representative
Section on
Men

"I require three things in a man. He must be handsome, ruthless and stupid."

—Dorothy Parker

WITH THE RIGHT TRAINING, THERE'S ALWAYS HOPE.

Men *do* have their uses, of course, some of which are quite pleasurable. It's their role as a father where the ambiguity and general utility questions start to arise. I suppose, perhaps, that mothers could be partly to blame because they have mostly trained and molded them into this uselessness. You would think that fathers would respond well to the whining, pleading, and sarcasm doled out by their children; they have already been trained first by mother, and then by wifey. Yet they seem to be deaf at most times, particularly when there is some sort of cleanup involved.

Many men have this strange affliction: they cannot abide "mess" from their children in the form of popsicles in the living room, markers on the rug, or Pixy Stix powder anywhere. Yet this is the same individual who thinks nothing of leaving his dirty underwear on the bathroom floor and cups half filled with cold coffee sitting on the oak desk in the office, and walks through the house with his shoes on after having just mowed the wet lawn.

More often than not fathers are reduced to the role of a glorified Mother's Helper. This is the rule rather than the exception, particularly in the land of Supermom. However, with a little creativity you can get your money's worth out of the sperm donation. There are some basic roles which you will need them to fulfill.

The Empty Threat—"Wait 'Til Your Father Gets Home" was a popular television cartoon when I was a child. And it wasn't meant in a sarcastic way at the time. Nowadays, if most women are like me, we trot this phrase out when we simply can't deal with the latest disaster that our young charges have laid upon us. An example of this timing would be when the only punishment which comes to mind involves altered birth certificates. Not the parentage, but the gender. The problem, however, can be that by the time the great savior comes through the door, the last thing he will want to do is be the bearer of discipline, not because his children are too precious to him, but because he is as shit tired as you are at the end of the day. A little training in the "You don't know what it's been like around here" mode is generally required. By the time you get to the third anecdote, they will relish the idea of escaping from your voice and whipping through a quick time out with Junior.

Men can haul heavy things. With a baby, you will require many heavy things. The stroller, the playpen, the case of beer, the highchair, etc., etc. Of course, they will likely carry these things without much complaint, but when you try to foist a twenty-pound wriggling baby on them, all of a sudden, the remnants of an old canoeing accident will suddenly begin to pierce their shoulder blades. Holding the baby exacerbates only this one area, funnily enough. Expect you will be the primary baby carrier in the family, so ensure all other lifting is left to him. There is no easy way to move a baby swing from room to room, believe me.

Men can often reach high things. This trait is not to be dismissed due to a height challenge—what do you think wobbly ladders were made for? Light bulb replacement, retrieval of helium balloons, socks on top of cupboards, and the like. For some reason, my husband seems to think he is the only one in the house who has the technological capability to replace light bulbs. Never mind that I wired the stereo, programmed the VCR, and continue to be the only person who can play back the video camera on the television.

He is an extra driver in the household. All of the jokes you hear about parents turning into little chauffeurs for their children are sadly true. You need the additional set of wheels on particularly busy weekends. Just remind him he can pick up a coffee while he's out, and he'll go. The downside to having them participate in driving the children around is: a) listening to his snide remarks about the discarded wrappers, toys, clothes and diapers in the car, and b) the discovery that this is the one place where baby cannot escape and is likely to sleep. Supermoms should learn to play the "I'll drive" martyr card for as long as they can, never letting on that this is a much better alternative than staying at home with the other maniac children.

Men can start the sentences only you can finish properly. We just need that lead-in sometimes.

Taking out the garbage seems to have a manly spin to it, don't you agree? I think it's because secretly they like to ensure that: a) we're not throwing out anything of theirs without telling them, and b) they can take the opportunity to throw out things of ours and the children's they deem unnecessary. A deflated SpongeBob SquarePants favorite ball comes to mind, as does the accompanying twelve hours of hysterics. Make sure you get them to stick to this chore by offering to bring the empty bins back into the house.

Men won't cook over a stove, but are more than willing to *barbecue*. Perhaps it's the obligatory beer in one hand, tongs in the other, or the inherent threat of an explosion. I know of a Supermom who works in a professional capacity, has birthed three children, holds an engineering degree, and she refuses to light a grill due to her safety concerns. It's her husband's job. Even if you're the type of Supermom who is not afraid of grilling, and do so quite often, there will be many times when you are relegated to the inside chores. This involves racing around like a madwoman in the kitchen preparing the other eighteen elements of the dinner which are needed, minding the children, answering the phone, refereeing arguments, re-installing the cable, and waiting for Mr. Wonderful to waltz in with his two slightly sizzled steaks and announce "Dinner's ready" to his admiring fans. He will then proceed to state "It's good, isn't it?" at least three times during the meal, at which you will be obligated to smile encouragingly at least once in order to stroke his sad little ego.

They aren't great self-starters, these fellows, but the great thing about most of them is that they do take direction. When my daughter was four, she announced to me that she was going to marry her two-year-old brother. When I asked her why, she said "He does what I tell him to." Frankly, a great quality to find in a husband. You go, girl!

ENDING IT ALL—WHO GETS THE SNIP?

Supermoms often feel their lives are out of control. One place you can take control is literally in your husband's pants. At many Supermom dinner parties, the conversation will frequently turn to one overriding subject: Sex. You and your husband are not alone in your quest to once again have sex on a regular basis. Children, home renovations, work, and children are the main reasons you are not "getting any." The conversation then quickly turns to the "side effects" of sex: more children, which would broaden the vicious circle. We all know (even men, although they are loathe to admit it) that there are significant health risks should a woman stay on birth control pills until she reaches menopause. We can all agree that condoms are best left to the youths of the world so, in a monogamous relationship where sex is not being performed for procreation purposes, there are limited choices. We want something permanent and relatively pain-free. We want, Supermoms hear me roar, our husbands to get a vasectomy. The mere thought strikes unparalleled fear into all husbands. They've heard of those mythical men who have had it done, and not only lived to tell but had a working penis afterwards, but they don't know who they are.

Men can be so clueless. What they fail to realize is that their argument about the pain involved with a vasectomy is being presented to a woman who has gone through childbirth at least once. It's like comparing a paper cut to open heart surgery. The only driving motivator these men have is that they could potentially get some sex at the end of the deal. Luckily, this is basically the only motivator they need—use it. If they dare use the argument, "But what if we divorce and my new wife wants children...," suggest using the "home vasectomy kit."

It is difficult and inappropriate to compare the risks and pain associated with a woman having her tubes tied versus a man having a vasectomy. Everyone has a different pain threshold, and to compare two surgical procedures from a pain perspective is nearly impossible. However, even a male friend admits the most painful part of his vasectomy was when he was putting his clothes away in the locker at the doctor's office, and he whacked his head against the sharp metal edge. After the "surgery," he bravely went on to the theatre that night, a bag of frozen peas clasped tightly in his lap. This is a real man.

The way I figure it, if you have more than one child, they actually owe you more than one vasectomy; there had better not be any complaints about the first.

There are "horror" stories about men who have had vasectomies, only to discover that their wives are pregnant mere months later. Unfaithful wives? No, ridiculous husbands are usually to blame. The sperm needs time to "get out," even after the procedure is performed. *"You mean my fellas can live longer inside the house than in the front yard?"* Strange but true. Not the living sperm part, but that men do talk this way. Apparently, it is more demeaning to "release" the fellas into a cup for re-testing than it is to a) have the vasectomy in the first place, or b) have another child. I have heard there must be at least twenty ejaculations before the pipes are clean. The good news is that we Supermoms do not have to be present for any of these goings on, should we so choose.

So get with it, men, and just remember...sex sex sex. It'll get you through the darkness.

PART 4:

Being a
Supermom
Would Be
a Lot Easier
without
Children

"Learning to dislike children at an early age saves a lot of expense and aggravation later in life."

—Robert Byrne

NOT EVERYONE IS A "KID" PERSON

This is not a shocking statement, particularly within the Supermom crowd. Our childless managers, competitive coworkers and wild single friends remind us of this fact each time we attempt to tell a charming anecdote about our angels. However, what may be a highly guarded secret is that even some of us Supermoms are not really "kid" people. You know you're one of them if you wouldn't cross a room to see someone else's baby. This is not because you are "kidded" out. You were probably like this before you had children. You like your own children just fine, but you're not so crazy about other peoples'.

The stark truth is that you can usually think of things you'd rather do with your jam-packed Supermom schedule than to make conversation, or hang out, with other people's children. It's not even because you think they're worse than your own in any way—behavior, intelligence, manners, etc. As a Supermom, you have to put up with your own children's bad behavior all the time, and you learn to take the bad with the good. There's nothing more frustrating to a Supermom, however, than watching inappropriate behavior from another child and not being able to do anything about it. This is especially true when dealing with an avid Homer whose "child blinders" are firmly in place. A stern look when no one is looking is the best way to go with these little brats. Supermoms have to be careful, lest they are accused of not knowing how to deal with children at all.

It comes as a surprise to Supermoms that children are people too, and as such, they have their own likes and dislikes, and frankly it can take a lot of time and effort to know other people's children and to appreciate their point of view. It's hard enough to get inside the heads of your own children (between 7:00 p.m. and 9:00 p.m. each night), and the mind of your husband (it's there somewhere), to worry about adding this to your agenda.

Supermoms are generally considered to be nice to other people's children—you give them popsicles, help them wash their hands, tease their brothers—especially when they like to do exactly what your children like to do. You are capable of feeding them, cleaning them, and entertaining them, but only when absolutely necessary.

There are "kid" people who don't have kids of their own. These are the friends Supermoms want to make and hold onto. When they come to your house, they don't bring along an annoying brood of their own, yet they're more than happy to bounce your baby on their lap, play with your three-year-old at the kitchen table, and to even give a bottle to an infant every once in a while. They're golden. Most of these folks will one day have children, if they're able, and then the novelty of your children will wear off pretty quickly.

It is totally understandable why some people don't want to have children. It's not for everyone. Many of them think the worst part about having a baby is the poo. It's not a great part, but frankly the giving up of an entire way of life is a little bit more invasive.

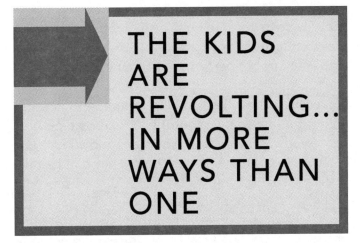

THE KIDS ARE REVOLTING... IN MORE WAYS THAN ONE

Supermoms exist in a sterile, clean, organized, and shiny environment. That is, maybe at work, but at home? Babies are pigs. Let's just get that out in the open right now. Yes, they're gurgly and sweet and the backs of their necks smell great...unless they have that cheesy, two-day old formula/breast milk smell to them. At any given time, there is stuff coming out of every orifice on a baby. From earwax to runny poop, they have it all. The phenomenon of seeing poo on the back of the baby's neck is, sadly, not an urban myth.

Ask any Supermom and they will have a million poo stories, snot tales, and pee adventures. Some of them are quite humorous, particularly when they happen to someone else. Every Supermom has a "spit up on my best suit" story to share.

Babies love to perform "the bounce and poo," or the "jump and dump." Essentially, whenever placed in any walker, saucer, jumping apparatus, swing, or anything requiring straps, babies will have a bowel movement. They just know.

Diapers are a wondrous thing. They can be tidy little packages, or full of wonderful surprises. In fact, there are many different types of diapers, all of which can be experienced in the course of one short day, with one little baby. Supermom classification levels are as follows:

1) A soaker—filled with urine, but thankfully nothing else.

2) A leaker—overfilled with urine, but thankfully nothing else.

3) A filler—filled with Number Two. Deadly when combined with the leaker.

4) Total Body Experience—you get the picture. The neck thing.

In our attempts to forego the diaper messes, which is relatively small in the scheme of things, we attempt to toilet train our darlings. Supermoms are known to look forward to this childhood milestone with the expectation that waste will cleanly and neatly be expelled into a waiting toilet. Wrong.

Get ready for the urine-fest and the fine art of wiping someone else's bum—a bum that is usually squirming and wiggling about in an attempt to shake loose any strays. Supermoms are advised to stick with the diapers as long as they can—at least there's some containment. A poo in the diaper is one less suit to take to the dry cleaners.

The good news is that practically everything washes out from whatever end it comes out of. Use a receiving blanket precaution with a baby known for spitting up, and take it as it comes. Passing the baby to a nearby spouse or obscure relative (kindly looking strangers will do in a pinch) at any time can cure this problem.

But never fear, Supermoms, there is an upside to all of this—you can now blame your pint-sized stain maker for all of the stains you make yourself. Every Supermom has walked around with schmutz on her shoulders at some time. You will discover that it is generally better to have the baby with you when explaining the mess, and that it isn't some foreign substance oozing from your head.

Little hands collect muck and germs. Keep a box of wet wipes in your kitchen, in a sealed plastic bag in your glove box, in the diaper bag, in your purse...you get the idea. If you haven't bought shares in a company that produces wet wipes, you may want to do so now. Supermoms know there's not much a wet wipe can't clean up. Expect the worst (i.e. actual poo on your best silk blouse). Anything less is gravy.

Kids are also revolting in the "declaration of war" sense. Why are they at war, and with whom? You, their resident Supermom. At any given time, in any given place, most of Supermom's children will be mad about some evil deed that's been perpetrated. Supermoms will find themselves at the receiving end of tantrums on a fairly frequent basis. A typical day might be:

The one-year-old is mad at you because you duct-taped his pastry brush. Apparently he doesn't share your view that sticking the broken bristles back in the wooden handle twenty seven times is enough, already. He is also mad that you hide the glue, disapprove of using a toilet for a handwashing basin, and generally frown upon eating sticky chocolate cookies on the new leather couch. Combine all of this with the fact that he believes he knows over two thousand words in the English language, and he has dense parents that only comprehend about three, and you've got yourself one red-faced little toddler. It is kind of like dealing with a messy drunk most of the time.

The four-year-old is mad at you because you won't let her wear shorts outside in the winter, you can't get her socks on at precisely the right angle, and you "chose" her to be a girl, instead of a boy, like her big brother. She's also incensed that you have cut off her attempts to pee standing up, you make her change her (boy's) underwear at least once each day, and because she can't have a sleepover every night of the week with her siblings. Additionally, your insistence on the unreasonable demand of brushing her teeth every day is really starting to wear.

If you have slightly older children, your ten-year-old son is likely to be mad at you because you forgot his hockey jersey and socks in the laundry room at home, making him twenty minutes late for his last game. If you insist on washing these items once a month, you will cause trouble. He's mad because you insist on knowing exactly why his teacher will be calling that evening, because he can't play his Nintendo on the big TV in the family room all the time, and because buying eighteen pairs of gloves every winter is such a big deal. Your ignorance of the video game memory card in the pocket of his balled-up jeans at the bottom of his laundry basket is pretty annoying, also. And your refusal to pay him for "being good" is nothing short of child abuse.

Your twelve-year-old daughter is furious with you for not supporting her pseudo-vegan lifestyle and being mean enough to make her eat meat at least twice a week. Your refusal to do laundry on demand, insisting that at least one piece of her bedroom carpet is visible under the clothes, and enforcing the no-dessert-in-bed rule really puts her over the top. Making her attend school on half-days, not allowing her to purchase CDs with parental warning labels, and not having "something decent to eat" in the cupboard all the time are also crimes you may have perpetrated against her. Most of all, though, she is mad that you chose to have three other children after reaching perfection with her. That, and the fact that you deliberately make nasty dinners every single night, and occasionally appear to know something she has no knowledge of, is really too much to take.

To top it all off, your husband is mad because you let the children tie together 150 hair elastics and dangle innocent stuffed animals over the banister at the end of an endless day off from school. He's mad that the children aren't as well-behaved, or as absent, as the two in Mary Poppins, and he's especially wound up because you allowed dessert-eating on the new leather couch...using the sticky chocolate cookies as spoons. He's mad that he doesn't get to spend enough time kayaking, playing tennis, shopping at Home Depot, and maybe just once he could take his massive SUV "off-roading" on more than a speed bump at the Starbucks parking lot.

If you weren't so crazy about all of them, you might start to take some of this kind of personally. Battles with your children are inevitable, but tough nonetheless. The tests of strength and endurance (mental and physical) are an ongoing struggle not often recognized by the outside world. Fear factor has nothing on being a Supermom. Magician David Blaine thinks he's pretty tough, having survived being suspended in a glass box for forty-odd days, with no food or facilities, while being ridiculed by passing Englishmen. Ha! If he really wants to test his strength and stamina he should try staying at home with children during a snow day.

As hard as your children will pray for "Snow Days" at the sight of the first snowflake, Supermoms are advised to frantically "counter-pray" in a futile attempt to offset their fervent wishes. Once in a while, the dreaded snow day arrives. After battling with your husband for forty-five minutes over who has the most important meetings of the day, losing the battles, and spending another forty-five minutes on the phone canceling your own sixteen meetings, you are faced with spending the day in a house full of children. Your children.

What to do, what to do. Do they: a) sleep in, or b) watch television until their eyeballs bleed, or c) lounge about in a state of perpetual boredom? None of the above. They awaken thirty minutes earlier than they are normally roused for a school day, eat a healthy breakfast in record time, find all their snow gear and get themselves out of the door faster than they've ever done for any school day.

(If you are a Supermom, you will have noticed several small miracles happening in that last paragraph: breakfast eaten without sugar or nagging, mittens where they should be, and leaving the house without the usual litany of complaints and arguments.)

Let the battles begin. Once the thrill of playing in the neighborhood snow pile (optimistically called "Snow Mountain" by my brood) has worn off, they settle in for a long day's fighting. Glass box? If it's soundproof, sign me up.

Additional tests of strength might include:

* Putting a snowsuit on a toddler who doesn't want to have a snowsuit put upon him. Completion without swearing (out loud) earns extra points.

* Finding two matching mittens for each of four children, for a period of at least one week. Resisting extra trip to Wal-Mart to supplement supplies, score one bonus point.
* Zipping up a ski jacket to the very top without catching a four-year-old neck fold in the process.
* Shoveling snow while the children "happily" play alongside.
* Shoveling snow while a preschooler rakes it back onto the driveway. Refrain from overused phrase "You're not helping" for added bonus.
* Making it through an hour of outside play without having to wipe your child's nose with your own mitten or bare hand.
* Getting a toddler out of their snowsuit, mittens, hat, gloves, and boots in fourteen seconds (the time lapse between when the urge to urinate hits them and before they can no longer hold it in). Luckily the snowsuit will be remarkably dry as they will have been outside for a grand total of one and one-half minutes.
* Explaining patiently to a surly twelve-year-old why, if the buses are not running, your personal car is also not able to take him to

his best friend's house. If completed without resultant slamming doors and "oh my god"s, score extra points.

If any challenger is interested in attempting these winter Supermom tests, it can also be arranged for them to experience a full list of spring, summer, and autumn exercises, which may or may not include the involuntary consumption of another human's bodily waste. Truly revolting.

ARTS & CRAPS

Supermoms are able to avoid many messy chapters in their child's life if the work schedule is demanding enough. Toilet training, the aftereffects of bad macaroni, and the lice checks come immediately to mind. Our fearless daycare instructors and nannies boldly march through many of these sticky, stinky, and sometimes disgusting activities. Another messy thing that is excellent to miss is arts and crafts time. Arts and crafts are, unfortunately, generally enjoyed by children of all ages. From a very young age, children are fascinated by painting, coloring, gluing, cutting, and anything that they can create with their own hands. This Supermom would like to meet the person who invented finger painting and made it part of the three-year-old-and-under arts experience. Then I'd like to shoot him. There is no single messier thing than finger painting, and it should be kept to places like preschools, play centers, and anywhere where you don't have to clean it up. Unfortunately, due to the overzealousness of our Homering counterparts, Supermoms are expected to be able to recreate many arts and crafts activities in their own homes. While most Supermoms won't have a fully stocked "Craft Cupboard," or even a shelf with an empty tape dispenser and two dried-up markers, your children will look to you to help fulfill their artistic needs.

When my daughter was two, all she wanted to do was paint. I discovered a sneaky way to keep this a clean activity. Give them regular construction paper, a big paintbrush, and a glass of water. That's it. Construction paper turns a darker color when wet, and you can convince your unsuspecting youngsters that they have special "disappearing paint" when the picture dries. Keeps the paper around a lot longer.

Gluing is a particularly messy sport, and should be confined to at least the kitchen table area. Kids' non-toxic glue is best. Give your child a sheet of paper and smaller pieces of paper to glue on to it, and they'll be at it for hours. To save the dumping of the whole glue bottle all at once, pour a little into a bathroom cup, and give them a cotton swab to spread it around. Just make sure it doesn't end up in their ear and everything should go smoothly.

Now comes the dilemma of where to display these works of art. Anyone who has more than one child can tell you that you will never be able to keep it all. Keep the pieces that you like (maybe two pieces per year), and put them in a scrapbook. Others you can take photos of, or discreetly "hide" in the garbage can when they're not looking.

Dads don't *get* artwork. They don't get why it's so important. It's just a big messy exercise as far as they're concerned. When it's done at school and makes its way home, they'll throw it in the garbage where the youngster is likely to spot it. Amateurs. Keep all artwork away from the men if you want to avoid a meltdown when your child discovers that their masterpieces have been thrown out.

Supermoms shouldn't pretend to know what their child has painted or drawn. It incenses them if you guess wrong. There is nothing inappropriate about asking them what it is, or just complimenting them on their use of color or brushstrokes. Sometimes a picture isn't of anything—it just made them feel good to create something. It's only as adults that we think every action we take has to have an end goal. Or, to put it another way, just be thankful that their math skills are looking good.

THE MOST ANNOYING QUESTIONS YOUR CHILDREN WILL EVER ASK YOU

1. What do you do all day?

2. Why can't you do laundry every day? Can't you just buy me more new clothes?

3. Do I have to eat this? Do I still get dessert if I don't? How come you make such disgusting things? Do you try to torture us?

4. Why isn't there a Kid's Day? How come there's a Mother's Day? A Father's Day?

5. How come Jane's mother doesn't have to work? Doesn't Daddy make enough money? Don't you like the other mothers? Don't you want to hang out with them?

6. Don't you like staying at home with me? Do you like meetings better?

7. Do I have to go to school? How much longer? What kind of job can you get if you don't finish school? McDonald's? What's wrong with that? Is there something wrong with people who work at McDonald's?

8. If I eat half my potatoes can I have dessert? Did you make dessert? How come you didn't make dessert?

9. Why do I have to go to bed? Why don't you stay up all night? What if I don't go to sleep and just stay awake? Can I have a later bedtime?

10. Do I have to get up? Are you sure? How come you let me go to bed so late?

11. Do I have to take a shower/bath? Didn't I just have one on Monday? Was Monday that long ago? Do I smell? Who'll notice?

12. Is it the weekend? It just finished? Is there school? Did it snow? Is it cancelled?

13. Why?

14. Is there a bathroom here? How come you didn't tell me to go before? Did you bring a change of clothes? Can we buy some new ones?

15. Is he adopted? Does he have to be my brother? Why did you have him? Can't you see how annoying he is?

16. Why can't I have a dog? A cat? A bird? A ferret? Why won't you be nice?

17. Do I have to wear gloves? My hat? My boots? My winter coat? Underpants?

18. Can we go bowling? To the funfair? To the mall? Why don't we ever do anything I want to do? What could *you* possibly want to do?

19. Are we there yet? How much farther? Why are we going here? Why did I have to come? Do we have to go home now?

20. How many days until Halloween? Christmas? My birthday? School ends?

THE BIGGEST LIES
WE TELL OUR KIDS

1. Santa Claus, The Tooth Fairy, and the Easter Bunny.

2. Your face will stay like that.

3. I know everything you get up to, so don't even try it, mister.

4. Shhhh—she's not fat, she's just big-boned.

5. Of course that's a lady, not a man.

6. I love all my children the same.

7. Daddy and I aren't arguing, we're just having a discussion.

8. Your brother isn't a butthead.

9. Those pants look perfectly fine on you. No, they're not too short. Let's go.

10. If we're late again, they'll throw you out of school.

11. I'm sure teachers work very hard on the Professional Development days. Yes, most teachers also leave the school at 3:30, but I know they go home and work some more.

12. Yes, going to college was well worth it to get the job that I have. I use everything I learned, *especially* trigonometry.

13. The neighbor's kids are very nice, they're just a bit different from us.

14. We don't have the money to buy junk food.

15. 8:00 is the universally recognized bedtime for all seven-year-olds. If you don't get enough sleep you will fail school.

16. If you don't take a bath at least once a week, potatoes will grow behind your ears.

17. No, I'm not mad at your father for being late again, I'm just disappointed he's missing dinner with us.

18. Oh, look, the pool is closed this weekend. Darn, I was looking forward to getting out my swimsuit again.

19. I would play that game with you, but I'm afraid I'd win.

20. I was thin until I had you children.

21. You'll love broccoli when you're older.

22. Don't think of it as eating a dead cow.

23. No, I don't think that boys who take ballet are sissies.

24. Daddy's mom is really nice to us, isn't she?

25. Christmas will be here before you know it.

26. I bet all of your friends are in bed already.

27. You looked really good in that jazz dance recital. No, I didn't notice that you tripped.

28. Stop laughing—I think your cousin's hair looks nice dyed blue.

29. I guess that three-year-old is still using a pacifier because he's not feeling well today.

30. No, I won't be the one who is embarrassed when you're still wearing diapers in kindergarten.

HOLIDAYS ARE HELLISH DAYS

It is hard enough for Supermom to get through a regular work week, let alone make it through any sort of holiday or celebration. Somehow we are expected to come up with "spare time" to participate in some unnecessary and usually annoying rituals. For example, Halloween. The one word, besides Christmas, that can strike fear into a Supermom's heart weeks before the official night of scaring begins. Every Halloween is the same: You've got fake blood all over your last pair of clean pants, the baby's nose is running like a river, your elder daughter is holding a pair of red shorts for stitching up ("I need them today!"), and the toddler is helping herself to Jell-O for breakfast. Oh, and you have the biggest presentation of your life tomorrow morning, which you need to begin writing tonight.

When did Halloween become such a big deal anyway? It used to be acceptable to have Mom's mascara, some fuzzy ears, and a pillowcase as our only accessories. Now it's all about perfectly traced and carved pumpkins, elaborate light-up costumes, light-up matching candy bags, decorations to rival Christmas, and all the while the main purpose—i.e. the candy bar—has shrunk to such Lilliputian size as to be ridiculous.

To children, Halloween is second only to Christmas in terms of appeal. The ability to go to virtual strangers' houses and get candy has a certain illicit, cheap thrill to it. Most kids wonder why parents wouldn't want to hold Halloween every night; it's such fun for everyone involved.

There are always families who refuse to give out any of the good candy—i.e. the store-bought, name brand, tiny little chocolate bars. What's with the granola bars and fruit snacks? Kids can get these out of the cupboard at home. Self-promoting dentists like to hand out toothbrushes. Sickos. I've heard of a family who hands out little packages of tissues—cleaning out the sample cabinet at work, I suppose. Get this straight. Halloween is about candy. Masses of bad-for-you, rot-your-teeth-out, no-nutritional-value-whatsoever candy. They're only kids once, so even Supermom has to let them have this one night. Don't even chase away the thirteen- to fifteen-year-old crowd. They'll have plenty of time to be old and "act their age."

The nanosecond Halloween ends, Christmas seems to start. The stores fill up their shelves on November first, and it's a bit off-putting in terms of purchasing something. You don't want to give them the satisfaction of doing your Christmas shopping in November simply because they've started putting out the merchandise for it.

Christmas for Supermoms is when we really get to either strut our stuff, or work ourselves to a mental breakdown. Between buying the decorations, hauling out the raggedy artificial tree, decorating the tree, the halls, the windows, cooking the turkey, baking the cookies, making sure the Christmas CDs are working, buying the gifts, wrapping the gifts, stuffing the stockings, and writing and mailing all the cards to friends and family, it's surprising there aren't more husbands found dead with a Christmas Angel stuffed down their throats. Every year, Supermoms address all of the Christmas envelopes, decide who is "lucky" enough to receive a photo of the children, put a stamp and return address label on each envelope, and then hand less than half the pile to their husband to complete. His half will represent people that are "his" friends and family. His cards always go out late, and he always gets heaps of praise from his mother about how he sent out the cards "himself." Congratulations.

When your children are young, they still believe in Santa Claus. This is a great leverage tool for Supermom. Use it well, and use it often. When you're ready to purchase the gift "from Santa," have your children write him a letter (or write it for them depending on age), listing their choices. Then tell them they can't alter the list. Convince older children that an intervening email will not do anything. Supermoms barely have time to purchase the first gift their children choose, let alone the twenty-seven items which come along once the catalogues and television ads start pouring in with a vengeance.

There is nothing wrong with Supermom telling her children certain toys or items are too expensive for Santa to bring, or that his workshop doesn't create rocket launchers. Just because they ask for it doesn't mean they get it. Tell your kids that you've spoken with Santa and, unfortunately, he can't bring what they want because they ran out, but can Mommy get it for their birthday? This can work when the desired toy is sold out all over town. These same toys are always available after the first week in January.

Christmas is a good time for Supermoms to buy your children items they need and you have to purchase regardless. Things like underwear, socks, t-shirts, pajamas, sheets even. Any of these with their favorite character imprinted on them will be exciting and well worth the extra couple of dollars you might have to spend to get the branded item. Socks fit nicely into stockings, as do gloves, hair clips, pens, and other items you would probably have to buy during the year.

Try to set a limit on your Christmas spending, and to curb your cost per item on stocking gifts. Supermoms are often found at the mall on December 24th purchasing outrageously expensive items to make the day perfect for their child. Just remember that no child will remember a single item that they received in their Christmas stocking, even two days later. It's important that it is full at the time, but a fifty-cent plastic toy can be just as exciting as a ten-dollar item to a six-year-old child.

Supermoms should try not to expect good behavior from their children at Christmas. They're so excited on Christmas morning that they're about to explode into a million pieces. It's okay to slow things down once they're older by assigning a "Santa" to pick out a present one by one from under the tree and hand it out to the recipient. This won't work when they're under the age of six or so.

Toddlers and preschoolers tend to open every present they lay their eyes on. Instead of printing their name on the nametags, replace it with their picture, so they know which gifts are theirs. There is nothing quite so vicious as the wrath of a wronged sibling whose present has been erroneously opened by another. Or you can put everyone's picture on their specific presents, and the younger child can then take on the role of "Santa." They get a kick out of this and it gives them something to focus on other than their own stash of waiting gifts.

Candy is a very important part of Christmas, especially to a child. Let them eat the candy from their stockings (it's one day, come on), and then give them a tiny plate of Christmas dinner. They'll be too excited and stuffed with chocolate to eat much, so don't turn Christmas dinner into a fight over finishing their plate to get to dessert. Let them eat quickly and then get down from the table to play with their new toys. Even Supermom is allowed to take a break from ensuring the kids are getting all the right nutrients, just for one day. Think of it as a Christmas present to yourself.

After all, the one thing a Supermom would ask for is time, and any time that your children are happy, you've just bought yourself some happy time.

If you insist on the old fashioned tradition of writing thank you cards for gift givers who were not with you on the big day, be sure the task does not take on epic proportions. You can use one card to thank the same family for presents to all of the children, with them inserting their own name and gift received. It's the thought that counts. If you don't have them mailed by the end of January, give it up. Have your children make a long distance call instead.

The deeper meaning (the true meaning) of Christmas tends to get lost in all the commercial aspects. The same can be said of Easter. Easter is a marathon of hiding chocolates all over your house plus the mother lode payoff of the giant chocolate bunny/chick/egg that must accompany the little eggs. Only hide the eggs where you can be reasonably sure that if they are not found for six to eight months they will not do any permanent damage to their surroundings. You will find chocolate eggs that far into the future, believe me. With any luck, it won't be on the back of your mother-in-law's cream silk skirt (assuming you get along with your in-laws). Don't hide the eggs too well, or you'll forget how crafty you were, as you most likely hid them either at 11:00 the night before, or in the early morning hours in a mad dash.

If you discover Easter morning that you have unbelievably forgotten to hide the eggs the night before, send the eager kids back to their rooms, and shamelessly tell them you have to make sure the Easter Bunny has indeed finished hiding the eggs. If need be, embellish this by warning them that he is known to bite small children if interrupted. Race around, hurling eggs helter-skelter into shoes, vases, couches, corners, anywhere you can. Announce that the eggs are indeed hidden and that you have secured the premises from the vicious Easter Bunny. Eggs in the shoes are a bad idea. Two-year-old boys don't always notice chocolate lumps in their shoes. The carpet might never be the same.

Spring Break. Besides "Summer Vacation," and "Snow Day," few two-word phrases can excite children as much. Okay, "road kill" might be another. As Supermoms prepare themselves and their children for the upcoming annual "break" from school and routine, it is reasonable to wonder exactly who will be getting a break out of the week. It certainly won't feel like Supermom as she drags her two maniacal preschool children around the Wal-

Mart desperate for that last airplane treat and requisite sunhat. You know that things have gone too far at the point when you crouch down, look into your toddler's eyes, and earnestly say to him, "Run away. Now." That, plus thinking that getting his fingers stuck in the automatic door would truly teach him a lesson.

The washing machine will be running for the third time in as many days in order to ensure the 'tween's "cool" clothes are at the ready; the Game Boy cord for recharging batteries has apparently spontaneously combusted; the kindergartner is aggressively arguing the merits of wearing new sandals and shorts to school in below freezing weather, and the one-year-old has outgrown his efficiently pre-purchased swimming diapers...since yesterday.

The teachers, for sure, are getting a break from the daily grind. The school bus drivers, lunch monitors, patrol crossing guards, and of course the students themselves. Or so they think. The meanest teacher on her worst day is not as scary as a tired Supermom on the last day of spring break.

For Supermoms living on the periphery of the educational system it would seem that the word "break" can be interpreted in a couple of different ways.

The first meaning, as in "to break," can refer to one of the following:

* *Your patience* as you discover that each of your children has outgrown the skis/swimsuits/sandals/hockey skates/fill-in-the-blank required for the week's entertainment.
* *The bank* as you dig deep to purchase the above at full retail.
* *Your back* as you carry into the house the supplies needed to feed and entertain a gang of bored teenagers.
* *At least one fragile item* in your house as the kids attempt to rediscover the "no hockey in the house" rule.
* *Every speeding limit* if you are a working parent and must get to a spring break camp by 4:30 each evening, after arriving late from the 9:00 drop-off time that morning.

Of course, the word "break" can also mean to provide an unexpected windfall, or stroke of good luck to someone, as in:

* *The retailers* as they gleefully announce their "spring break madness" in February, and then jack up the prices of items you really need for that week one day before it starts.

* *The travel agents* and suppliers whose ticket prices escalate to astronomical amounts during that one week only.
* *House burglars and car thieves*, who scour empty residential "kid-filled" neighborhoods.
* *Owners* of movie theatres, bowling alleys, gymnastics providers, indoor playgrounds, private daycares, mini-camps, etc etc.
* *Airport vendors* with their rubbery hot dogs, $5.00 cups of stale coffee, and overpriced magazines and chocolate bars. Not to mention the $15.00 ceramic bell with "I Love NY" that your ten-year-old *has* to have.

The private schools also take this time to reinforce the little extras that their special students are getting, by allowing them to have a two-week break that always overlaps with the one week at public schools. Just to rub it in. Most children would opt for the stiff uniforms, extra homework and mono-sex institutions just to get this extra week off, given the chance. As the high tuition costs must mean that many families must be double-income to afford these schools, private school break means extra vacation time that Supermom has to take off.

The Supermom theory is that it must have been a secret coalition of teachers, travel industry providers, and camp operators who decided that

March is a super time to have a week free from school. So get your Visa ready—the plastic one, that is—and have a great break.

In the past, Valentine's Day was traditionally for secret admirers to notify the objects of their affections of their admiration. This is now akin to stalking or sexual harassment, and is not normally practiced. For Supermom, the romance of Valentine's Day quickly wears off. Each child arrives home with a list of his or her twenty-five schoolmates, and for each you must prepare a Valentine. Very politically correct. Don't miss anyone— including the teacher, the librarian, the gym teacher, the lunch monitor, the principal, and so on. You'll be the one to write them, and you'll be lucky if your children sign their names. Supermoms are traditionally known by the cheap store-brand ones; we like to mask our guilt by ridiculing the other mothers who make them by hand. The best Valentine's cards you'll receive will be the handmade ones from your children. You'll save them forever, and they're good to pull out when your children are in the pre-teen and teenage years and you hear more "I hate you"s than "I love you"s.

Supermoms *can* survive the holidays with children. All it takes is the precision planning of a sergeant major general at war, the budgeting skills of Scrooge McDuck, and the patience level of Mother Teresa. Just make sure you capture the good moments on film, or no one (including yourself) will believe that it actually happened.

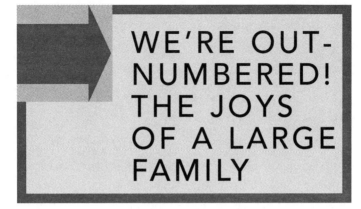

WE'RE OUT-NUMBERED! THE JOYS OF A LARGE FAMILY

Some Supermoms have more than the national average of 1.2 children. Superdupermoms, or just plain crazy? Back in the 1960s, it was commonplace for couples to produce four, five, even six children. Nary a neighbor would raise an eyebrow. Times have changed. To have four children causes many exclamations of surprise and incredulity from friends, coworkers, and especially bosses. You will be hard pressed to find friends willing to "go the distance" with you, with the exception of accidental multiple birth situations.

Most Supermoms are clearly frightened to go beyond the standard two. They're doing the math correctly and figuring out that they will be outnumbered. Adults, however, have a secret weapon.

We are bigger, smarter, and are "the boss," while the children are not. Some people haven't figured this out. The thought of yet another *dictator* in the house frightens them.

A first baby is overwhelming. So much work. So little time. So many demands. No one understands. Why would anyone add another to the household? Any former social life will come to a screeching halt so you may as well make it worth your while and pop out a companion for burden number one.

Ask any Supermom with multiple children, and she'll tell you that the work is all relative. If you have one child, having no children around is easy. If you have two children, you can do anything with one child. If you have three, two seems like a breeze. And so on, and so on. At a level of four children, a Supermom can do practically anything when only dealing with three children. One of the four will generally lessen the load the most, but don't reveal which one, in order to avoid some heavy therapy bills. Having many children around means great things, most of the time.

1) They always have someone to play with, fight with, be partners with, plot against Mom with, build forts with, and generally be a kid with.

2) They can share the blame for anything that gets broken. They *can* share it, but they rarely do, opting instead for an "every man for himself" approach.

3) As a parent, you can use one child's exemplary behavior against another. Nothing brings out the good qualities in a child quite as quickly as one of their siblings getting into trouble.

4) They can go to the park together. The odds of more than one breaking their neck on the monkey bars at precisely the same time are slim.

5) A nice, loud, interactive dinner table. You can't beat it.

Your house will feel empty when even one of the children is out. Maybe not empty, but a lot quieter. Socialization skills between siblings is unique. They beg you to sell their brother one minute, and in the next minute beg you to allow them to sleep in his room that night. You'll grow to love the sounds of children being raised. It's not quiet, it's not tidy, and all in all, it's not pretty, but ask anyone who grew up in a "large" family (four now being "large"), and they'll tell you how wonderful it was.

EVERY DAY IS A WHINE FESTIVAL

Managing a team at work and coming home to a house full of children is often like trading in one set of babies for another. Some people never grow out of whining. Many middle-aged adults, mostly parents, could count whining as a major activity in their day. Babies start slowly. Not the hysterical crying but the sort of fussing and whining they do for sport. They hone this skill until the age of about two, when the whining becomes their primary communication method. It is probably the most annoying thing about a two-year-old. When dealing with an only or first-born child, the whining may be minimal and more expunged. But if you have older children as role models, look out. The whining of a two-year-old is small potatoes compared to the screaming or whining of a twelve-year-old girl.

Children whine about the most absurd things:

* My socks hurt.
* The couch is stupid.
* My brother says if I were an animal I'd be a cat, and I don't like cats so it's not fair.
* I'll starve to death if you don't let me have that fourth cookie.
* The door to my bedroom doesn't close right.
* You always buy things for everyone else in the world except me.

The list is endless. Supermoms need to nip the whining in the bud early, or children will see it as an effective way to get what they want. Supermoms frequently give in to stop the insufferable noise. This is simply learned behavior from the office.

Like many annoying childhood traits (e.g. nose-picking), we are optimistic that the whining will disappear when the children realize how revolting this habit can be. This is not true. This doesn't normally happen. Grown people can be more irritating than their junior counterparts. The whining you hear from friends and strangers alike mostly centers around "work." Work at the office, work with their children, work with their spouse, work around the house, work for their parents...sheesh, no wonder they're tired. Supermoms are tired, too.

Most of our "work" is due to personal choice. You chose to have children, you chose to go further with your education (there may have been some undue parental pressure there, but it still counts), you chose to pursue a high-stress career, you chose to live in the house you do and buy the clothes you do (which require hand washing some of the time), and you chose the husband you marry. You chose this Supermom lifestyle. If you were to continually whine about these things, you'd really be criticizing yourself and the choices you've made. If you have made bad choices, then you should ask yourself, "What am I doing to change the situation?" If you're not doing anything about it then you have no right to whine.

There are few things in life that we truly have no control over. Death is one of them, place of employment is not. Aging is one of them, enrolling children in eighteen different lessons during the week is not. It's hard to figure out why people are whining sometimes. The $500,000 home renovation? Their choice. The caring of a widowed, elderly parent? Not their choice.

Whining can be a disguised form of bragging. "If only Johnny hadn't made the triple A hockey team, I wouldn't have to spend every day in an arena." "We get back from the ski trip one day and have to turn around the next to go to Florida. I'm exhausted." "My new job is so demanding." These, in my opinion, are the worst kind of whiners. Why can't these folks see the positive side of the activities and lifestyle choices they've made? Perhaps it's a commentary on our society in general that people believe they don't have the ability to change their lives. Similar to the person suing McDonald's because he got fat eating there four times a week; there is no sense of personal responsibility.

You don't like your job? Start looking for another one, train to get promoted, volunteer your time to explore new options. Housework gets you down? Relax your standards, employ your spouse and kids to take on their own chores, or, if you have the money, hire someone to do it for you. Feel like a chauffeur driving the kids to and from lessons and school? Drop one lesson per child and let them take the school bus if it's available. Find ways to not only make your dreams come true, but to realize that each day is a gift. Look for the best thing that happens to you each day. And stop whining.

AND IN THIS CORNER...

Supermoms take on many different roles, and one that they have to revert to quite often is that of referee. Fights are a way of life when you have children. The children fight with each other, with you, and with their father, and you fight with their father over the children. I'm not talking about physical violence, rather the verbal tirades we can unleash with incredible venom on those we love the most. Siblings are the worst. Perhaps proximity is to blame. Parents unrealistically assume their children will want to play together simply because they live in the same house.

When a child is young, she will look at an infant sibling with nothing but love in her eyes. The baby is "her baby" and she loves and protects this precious baby from any interlopers. In return, when said baby grows into a toddler, he will worship his older sister. In a cruelly ironic twist, however, as soon as the toddler is old enough to emulate his older sister and want to be with her every second, the older sister will decide she has had enough of Junior hanging around.

Some older siblings tend to maintain this air of superiority over their younger siblings even as adults. They take on the role of junior parent when Mom and Dad aren't around anymore. This can sometimes be a blessing, and sometimes a curse. Supermoms need to recognize that their own children may not grow into being good friends with each other as adults. Your job is to ensure that they respect each other's differences and see each other as human beings, not objects of derision and abuse, as they did in their younger days.

PART 5:

Some Handy
Information
for Supermom's
Infrequent and
Ill-Advised
Public Outings
with Her Own
Children

"I take my children every-where, but they always find their way back home."

—Robert Orben

INDOOR PLAY GROUNDS—STAIRWAY TO HEAVEN, OR HELL?

For the Supermom, the very idea of an indoor playground may seem like an evil scheme to separate them from their hard-earned money for an activity which can be enjoyed at no charge in the great outdoors. This is a misconception. Supermoms should embrace the indoor playgrounds as they are designed with parents in mind, not the toddlers, unlike outside parks and play areas. Outside there's sand, dog poo, broken glass, the threat of sunburn, candy wrappers, stinging nettle, flying insects, and nosy neighbors. Inside, there's fresh coffee, comfortable chairs, magazines, change tables, flush toilets, clean toys, and parents and children with whom we are mostly unacquainted. Naturally we're more polite and less nosy with people we don't know.

That being said, there are a few pitfalls of which to be aware. Oh, sure, it seems nice enough, with coffee brewing, bright new toys, and ample seating for ample childbearing bottoms. Look beneath the surface though, and you'll see what it's really all about. Homers practically live here, so beware.

Supermoms entering an indoor playground for the first time will encounter a wide variety of parenting styles that they may need to adapt to, but most likely just stay the hell away from. Luckily, you won't have to observe for long to identify each style.

1) The Overprotective Mother. It's a mystery why this type visits an indoor playground. Their entire visit is spent running after their spawn—helping them up and down eighteen-inch-long slides, ensuring that they say please and thank you to all of the other spaced-out toddlers, forcing them to share even when they are the only children interested in a particular object, and generally "stressing out" over how their child could hurt themselves on the evil play equipment. This particular mother (scientists have never been able to explain why this phenomena does not afflict men) easily morphs into her more evil cousin...

2) The "Queen of Dirty Looks" (a.k.a. *your* child is a philistine). Members of this sanctimonious breed often display the same traits as the overprotective mother with the added bonus of believing that their precious child has been doubly-blessed by the angels and as such should not have to be subjected to the machinations of other children. While stalking their innocent prey (i.e. *your* children), they will look for every opportunity to throw you the *"did you see what your devil child just did?"* look, as well as the "*isn't my child unbelievably wonderful*" glance at the same time.

3) The Phlegmish Crowd. A charming combination of carelessness and righteousness. Their children are easily identifiable by their open wounds, running noses, snot-caked faces, and smelly diapers. It makes every one of us want to take on the dirty look persona, if only for this one set of children. When the inevitable spill, spit up, or other expulsion of bodily fluid erupts from these children, the mother or father is most likely found "hiding" the evidence in some way—shifting the diaper bag over one inch to cover up the baby barf, moving the children from the poopy slide to a clean playhouse, etc.

4) The Barely-There Parent. A personal favorite. Most often manifested in the out-of-place dad or a

mom who is on at least child #3. (It takes time to develop this type of stress-free attitude. Although in the father's case, it's simply how they've acted from day one.) Most often these folks can be found lounging over coffee, reading papers, paying bills, chatting with others, and generally allowing their children to roam freely and learn the playground rules by themselves. Supermoms are encouraged to aspire to this level of independence, both for us and our children.

Occasionally, the operators of the indoor playground decide the plethora of toys isn't enough to raise children's excitement level to stratospheric heights, so they hire a big purple character to come in and wind them up even more.

Situations to avoid: Screaming "Why won't you dance?" into the face of your bawling child. "We're here to see him and you're going to get up and have some fun. I paid for this, you know!" Two-year-olds don't draw the parallel between a mother's deflated wallet and their own personal happiness. Many mothers (Homers and Supermoms alike) will forcibly move their screaming, kicking children through a crowd of other children to place them in the front row, which is clearly the last place they would like to be. Some Moms can't believe their children would let them down by not maniacally dancing around like all the others. They're just kids. If they want to see the character, they will. Otherwise, let them have fun in their own way. Some of them simply like to see the character in the background—we Supermoms can admit that up close some of them scare us a little bit too.

Singing characters and indoor playgrounds are all about the parents, and there's nothing wrong with that. The problem is that not all parents behave. Specifically, the mothers. From the overbearing to the apathetic, all breeds are represented here. Naturally your child will only steal toys away from the overbearing, oversensitive crowd, instead of the children whose mother spends the entire fun-filled hour talking on her cell phone and drinking coffee. Try to steer your children towards the latter for minimal impact as this mother is least likely to make a fuss about how your child infringed on her Little Precious' personal space by hurling a big plastic drill two feet in his direction. If you notice a mother walking around, pulling her child in a wagon, with her overstuffed diaper bag protectively slung over her shoulder and her two-year-old with a pacifier still firmly in place, stay away. These are hallmark signs of an overprotective, overzealous guardian of children. Who would brave a visit to an indoor playground to steal diaper bags?

Then there's the always-present pushing, yelling, hair pulling, and tripping to get to the big purple character in order to have pictures taken. These mothers need to control themselves. The children are towed along like reluctant baggage, to be plopped into the purple lap, and forced to smile. Never happens. This is a metaphor for mothering: perfect moments are never captured by anyone but yourself.

Children are unavoidably drawn to others of their type—other children, that is. As such, you will find yourself frequenting playgrounds and other meeting places of these creatures. There, you will lie in wait to judge the actions of others, and have your actions judged in turn. Fear not, for you have entered the world of competitive parenting the moment you place your young child on the playmat next to another, and await their charge towards the big, purple prey. It's not pretty, but it is inevitable.

MY CAR IS JUST A BIG PURSE

Few things can irritate a husband more than looking at the interior of a typical Supermom's car. On any given day he might find: an old coffee cup, two towels, a backpack, a grungy receiving blanket, a chewed up playing card, a sticky lollipop, a tube of lipstick, and an old McDonald's bag. It's a mystery as to how the stuff gets in there, and there's never a free hand to take pieces of it out each time you leave the car. Those Supermom hands are usually filled with grocery bags (kids need milk), soccer shoes (the fourth pair this season), and an overflowing briefcase full of good intentions. The towels are probably the husband's attempt to cover up the leather seating so the kids wouldn't get them sticky. Yeah, right. Unless they are superglued down, the towels won't stand a chance. They do, however, make handy tissues for explosive sneezes.

A Supermom normally manages to keep her car filled with gasoline past the quarter tank mark, at all times. This is mostly a female quality. Men love driving the car on empty, just to see how far they can go. The gas gauge is apparently the car manufacturer's opinion of how much gas is left. Don't even try to explain to your husband how much non-fun it would be to run out of gas with young children in the car. Unless the lights are flashing and there is actual sputtering, he will think you're overreacting. (The bastard never runs out of gas.)

Your car says a lot about who you are, and how young you feel. A real Supermom has a freakish aversion to a minivan, as it defines an image we spend most of our time fighting against—the Soccer Mom. Definitely not how Supermoms see themselves, *even when* every seat in the van is filled with a young child, and you're on your way to a soccer game, at which you will be a Mom. There may even be some Gap clothes being worn.

Supermoms can try the following van-avoidance technique: Convince your husband of two things: 1) that you don't need *two* big vehicles—one will suffice, as you only stuff your family in all at once on the weekends, and 2) wouldn't he look cool in a gargantuan Sports Utility Vehicle? If you're lucky, he'll buy the argument, and you'll have the zippy sports car while he drives the monster truck. If any of the children put on more than a couple of pounds in a year, the back doors on the car might not close very easily, but it'll be worth it in the pursuit of salvaging your Supermom ego. This is not a midlife crisis (that's for men only), simply a reality check.

EATING OUT WITH YOUR CHILDREN (IT CAN BE DONE!)

Supermoms are used to boorish table manners and inappropriate comments. After all, we've all been to at least one sales conference in the past year. But sitting with Ed "The Octopus" and Sam "The Spitter" while choking down rubbery chicken is nothing compared to taking your kids out to eat. Other people seem to think that the parents should take responsibility for their dinner performance. Taking your children out to a restaurant is a nerve-wracking experience. And by "taking out," this is not to be defined as any sort of restaurant with a Playplace attached to it. That's just an indoor playground with bad catering.

Supermoms frequently find themselves at fast-food restaurants (they are the ones badly disguised as a merchandising outlet for the hottest kids' movie). It's a done deal. Children as young as two can recognize a McDonald's sign from six blocks away. The appeal comes not from the meal, but from the "experience." The playing, the toys, and the bragging rights with their little friends.

Somewhere there is a mountain of unbiodegradable cheap plastic toys from McDonald's. Their limited appeal is precisely the amount of time you have allocated for your child to eat dinner. They haven't eaten the dinner, merely played with the cheap toy until it's time to go. There's only one solution: let them have the toy (or play in the play area) after they have eaten their meal. A hard one to enforce. Also, throw out the toys when you get home—no one wants to buy them in a garage sale, the parts are unsafe for the under-three crowd, and they seem to multiply while you're sleeping. The kids will never miss them.

If you feel like a real Supermom and decide to take on the challenge of eating at a real restaurant, make sure you consider each restaurant visit as practice for the times where misbehavior is definitely not an option (i.e. out with the in-laws or your Moms group).

1) Ensure you have a suitably stocked diaper bag for babies and a change of clothes for anyone

whose bladder control is suspect (could be you, the newly post-partumed Mom).

2) Bring small cars or toys the children have not seen for some time, which will entertain them for maybe ten minutes.

3) Take a pen or pencil and some paper for the older children. A child-friendly restaurant will have coloring placemats. If not, bring your own puzzle books or coloring books.

4) Make sure the children are good and hungry. Fasting for a couple of days never hurt anyone.

5) Let them choose their own meal off the kiddie menu, if they can. If they can't read it, then they're likely not old enough to have a meal to themselves. Share off your own plates and ask for some plain rice. Kids love rice, and the clean-up will belong to someone else! Same goes for ketchup—let them use as much as they want (you're paying for it, don't worry).

6) Let kids know where the washroom is. If they want to use it two to three times during the meal, let them; or even better, tell them how much fun it can be to play "Washroom Attendant" while earning extra cash.

7) Establish a seating plan where the children who are most likely to fight or bug each other are as far apart as possible. Use separate tables if required.

8) Order as soon as you can, or even as you leave the house. You may want to bring a take-out menu with you when you leave so that you can decide what you want before you go back the next time. The waiters will have served your dinner in record time to get rid of you, but it won't be fast enough. You will be skipping the coffee and dessert. Murderous looks from other diners, and the end of your own patience level, will preclude any after-dinner enjoyment.

9) Let the kids have their dessert even if you're on the main course. It will keep them happy at the table longer.

10) If you have children ten and over, let them sit together at a separate table, pretending to be grown-ups. They'll enjoy the chance to act responsibly, and you'll have a quieter table. Try to remember to take them home with you as the return trip to the restaurant is a drag.

Supermoms can successfully eat many meals in restaurants with their children. The real professionals avoid the following pitfalls:

1) Don't let your child wander around the restaurant, even if you are following him. It teaches the toddler that this is acceptable behavior. It isn't. It's unsafe (waiters tripping), and it

bothers the other patrons. If you want to follow Junior around, go home and do it.

2) Don't order more than one meal for your child. If she doesn't like what is put in front of her, same rules as at home. That's all she gets, or there's no dessert. Restaurant portions can be large, so have reasonable expectations about how much your children eat.

3) Don't order fancy Shirley Temple drinks. Take the drink that comes "free" with the kid's meal. Ask the waiter/waitress to put an orange slice or cherry in the drink.

4) Don't take your children to a restaurant that is clearly intended for adults only. Consider that a good majority of the people in the room are shelling out cash at home for a babysitter so they can get away from the little rats...they certainly don't want to spend the evening with yours.

5) Don't sit in the smoking section. Request a seat far away from it. Don't grin and bear it. Nothing is more irritating to a smoker, who is also paying money for their meal, to have an irate, sanctimonious parent ask them to put out their cigarette.

6) Finally, if your child is acting up (screaming, crying, throwing things, visiting other tables), please ask for a doggy bag and get out. Remind the

children to call you "Auntie" as you exit.

You'll spend about six times the amount it would have cost you to make the same food at home, but you've been able to delegate the preparation, serving, and cleaning up to someone else, without having to trade tasks later on in the week. This alone is worth the money. If the food was delicious too, you're doing great. Now maybe you're ready to take the kids to a movie...or maybe not.

FIELD TRIPS ARE FROM HELL

Supermoms fantasize about the strangest things in the middle of four-hour meetings with inadequate coffee. For example, attending a field trip with their children. In theory it's such a pleasant idea; you and your youngster, rosy-cheeked and smiling, enjoying an outing with his little friends, pleasant teachers, building camaraderie with the other parents. Ha. If your children are under five, they will undoubtedly perform one of the following tricks during your trip:

1) Need to go to the bathroom at the most inconvenient time—i.e. after Farmer John has painstakingly gathered everyone into a barn stall the size of an office cubicle, lined all of the children up by size, and has waited patiently for all of the pushing and giggling to stop, in order to demonstrate milking. The only washroom is an outhouse (which they will refuse to go into once

you're there), which you passed by the front gate fifteen minutes ago.

2) Behave in a bratlike manner—either kicking, pushing, swearing, or insulting Mommy just so that the most sanctimonious of all of the other parents, or teachers, can see and hear. You must then mutter "She's never done that before" to an unbelieving crowd.

3) Pick their nose and look for somewhere to hide it. Inevitably on their bus companion, who is naturally you.

4) Make some comment about the size (if some-what overweight) or fashions (if severely outdated, or alternatively very trendy) of one of the teachers or mothers.

5) Insist on going back home the minute you arrive at the designated fun area. They like the bus ride the best; most nursery school outings should simply *be* a bus ride.

Now, if your children are a few years older, they will still encourage you to attend a field trip with them (unless you have embarrassed them by speaking with the class geek on the last trip, or regaled their friends with tales of their babyhood). Once the actual trip is in progress, however, they will have nothing to do with you. They accept that they will be placed into a group headed by you, but

God forbid you should enter into any conversations with them or their group-mates. They will not sit next to you on the bus or at the venue itself. You may find yourself at a horrible medieval lunch/festival event surrounded by parents you don't want to get to know, while your daughter yuks it up big time with her pals in front. Amazingly, your older children will not find you witty, amusing, or in the least bit cool to hang with, so don't even attempt to chill with them. They just need to know that you're there, I suppose.

Another wonderful side effect of attending a school trip with your children, besides seeing how they act with their friends (frightening though that is), is the opportunity to hear firsthand how your own parenting skills are suffering. Listening in to the typical type of parents (i.e. Homers, who else) who go on field trips can be disheartening. As a side note, there is always at least one dad in attendance on these trips, whom all the mothers will speculate about in group whispers, how wonderful he is to make the time, or alternatively what a deadbeat he must be if he doesn't have a job to go to during the day. The rest of the Homers' time will be taken up talking about grades, school projects, all of the extracurricular classes their children are enrolled in, what their natural talents are, how much they have grown in the last year, what the teachers for next year are supposed to be like, how the principal annoys them, etc., etc. This is the land of the truly obsessed. Supermoms will be paranoid about being lumped in with the rest of them, so you will make it a point to indicate that you're either on a day off work ("such short notice, always tough"), or on a maternity leave (cue loud talking about "the baby" at home). You will desperately need these women to know that you have another life. Why this is so, we don't know. They say that we're most afraid of/angered by the people that we fear we ourselves will turn into. Eek.

So the next time you have a field trip coming up, please go, but remember that once you strike up an over-the-bus-seat conversation with someone, you're fair game for dissection and analysis on the next round.

DO YOU REALLY NEED A PICTURE OF THAT?

A strange phenomenon has overtaken many a Supermom in her neverending quest to capture the scarce and precious times she spends with her children. It is not enough to savor these moments in person, she must record it in some way. This generation of children will be the most photographed, videotaped, and recorded generation in the history of mankind. It is not possible to attend a $2.00 puppet show without overanxious parents whipping out their video cameras or digital cameras to capture the look on Junior's face when he finally looks like he's having a good time. Supermoms (and Homers too) should ask themselves this question—if it's boring when you tape it (e.g. thirty minutes of a child's swimming lesson), why do you think it will be any more interesting when you watch it on tape? *Will you watch it on tape? Who would?*

Most of our lives are not video-worthy, yet we persist on attempting to capture mundane moments, as if we're afraid we'll forget them as soon as they're over (okay, a real risk, but in the overall scheme of things...). Do try to capture *some* non-special moments like raking the leaves, eating dinner, going for a walk, playing at the park, riding bikes. These are the times that we'll likely forget as we grow old. They're the most interesting moments to look back on when the kids are grown. It shows us the lifestyle we really had, instead of fake smiles and once-worn dresses at Uncle's Jack's sixty-fifth birthday party. Not to say that it isn't important to capture on video their own special moments at their first birthday, Christmas, Halloween, etc., as well. *Note to self: ensure fourth child's first birthday coverage is as extensive as first, or there will be therapy bills later.*

Photos are another potential evil. When you're taking a picture of Little Precious, please bear in mind that the rest of us have little to no concern as to how that photo is going to turn out. The world will not stand still while you align a squirming toddler. Parents will get themselves into all kinds of contortionist positions, make odd noises, and generally make total asses out of themselves in order to get Johnny in a "natural" pose. Take a photo of him with his finger up his nose—now that's normal for a two-year-old.

Record the moments where you best see your children as they really are. And make sure that both parents take turns operating the camera, as your children will want to see *your* funky styles in the years to come. Now smile…

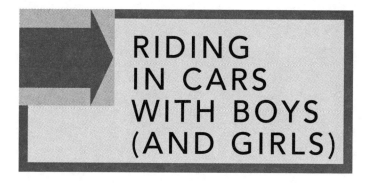

RIDING IN CARS WITH BOYS (AND GIRLS)

When Supermom looks for a way to relax after a hard week's work, she might have a momentary lapse of sanity and opt for a car ride. In the past this would evoke images of Dad in a sporty cap, Mom laughing beside him with her scarf gaily floating in the breeze, and the two children, rosy-cheeked and immaculately groomed, sitting properly in the backseat. Think 1950s Oldsmobile commercial. Fast forward fifty years. The car is just as likely to be driven by women as men (another victory for equal rights, I think), or maybe a realization by the men that this is the "working" part of the holiday. Many Supermoms do the majority of the driving, while Dad snoozes in the front seat, and the back seat is reminiscent of a battle scene from WWI, complete with blood, dirt, and gore.

Babies normally love to travel in the car; however, it is also their favorite spot to develop one of their more charming habits, that of spitting up, or sneezing a "wet one" and rubbing it all over their face. Also, a baby who can calmly keep her pacifier firmly ensconced in her rosebud mouth for two hours straight while bouncing in the jolly jumper suddenly loses the suction power necessary to perform this great feat in a car seat. Supermom can discover contortionist skills of Cirque du Soleil proportions while attempting to find said pacifier in a rear-facing car seat. Ah, the good old days (about ten years ago), when you could strap the infant seat into the front passenger seat beside you. A real Supermom could bottle-feed, pacifier-stuff, wipe faces, and in a pinch change their clothes, without coming to a stop. I think it was people who don't have young children who created front air bags.

Toddlers in the car are a bit of a nightmare too. They start with the ritualistic kicking of the driver or passenger seat (depending on their placement), and graduate to the throwing of hard plastic toys at the back of Mom's head. They also discover that this is a good place to sit quietly, out of Mom's disapproving glare, and burrow into their nose for treasures.

Once they're past the age of four or so, children come to see the car as a wrestling arena, with their sibling as the hated opponent. In this corner we have little Janie, weighing in at forty-seven pounds, known for her ability to "look at" her opponents and send them into a frenzy of pain and anguish. In the other corner, we have Stinky Timmy, his nickname rightfully earned through his startling ability to pass the most foul smelling gas at free will. Most likely to happen when his sister's head is in his immediate vicinity. Let the battle begin.

"She's looking at me!"

"He's farting!"

"You're so stupid."

"Not as stupid as you."

"You're so stupid you don't know how stupid you are."

"Retard!"

"Mom!"

Sigh. And you're only at the end of the driveway. And this is after the obligatory seating fight prior to even entering the vehicle. You might want to create a multi-columned spreadsheet recording which child has sat in which seat on each car trip, with a long-term strategy embedded, dedicated to ensuring that all is "fair" (the word most overused by eight- to ten-year-olds) whenever you have to go out in the car. Besides an aversion to sitting in cold hockey arenas for hours, one of the major reasons a Supermom might not encourage her son to go into hockey is the thought of all of the car rides you would have to take to get him to said arenas.

If you're planning a long car trip with your children, prepare yourself. It will not be relaxing, unless there are over-the-counter pharmaceuticals involved. Now, if only the car manufacturers could design a vehicle with a sliding glass partition (à la some taxi cabs) so that you could really muffle the shrieking and whining...

SHOPPING WITH CHILDREN— YOU'LL DROP BEFORE THEY DO

Supermoms are generally women (or a reasonable facsimile thereof) and as such, predisposed to shopping. This love dies with the birth of children. Sure, shopping used to be a pleasurable experience. The thrill of searching for and finding just the right blouse, the right shoe, the right pillowcase, whatever it was it didn't matter. Like a hunter on a mission there was no such thing as too much shopping. Once you become a Supermom, this changes drastically.

Picture this: baby strapped into a "baby-friendly" gray plastic seat covered in gooey substances you don't want to look at too closely. This seat has the unique ability not only to block the entire view directly in front of your shopping cart, but also to shove the baby down further and further with each step you take. No matter how you bundle them up in their own clean receiving blanket, they'll find a way to chew on the ratty black restraining belt. You'll give up and allow them to do this by the time you reach the check-out. At most stores they will only have two carts outfitted with these special baby seats, which are a must if you need to purchase diapers, a case of formula, and other large items. Placing the baby car seat in the cart will take up the whole of the grocery cart, rendering the trip useless. Apparently, according to the greeter at the store, these carts get stolen. Huh? Pretty awkward stroller. It is more likely to be a master plan to keep squalling babies out of their stores to allow others to shop in peace. And this is at the Wal-Mart, not Chanel.

Besides the baby, it is de rigueur to have a two- to three-year-old toddler in tow. One who is predictably: a) wearing clothes you didn't realize he had on when you left the house and now have you mortally embarrassed, b) picking his nose and enjoying a light snack, and c) rushing towards everything in the store that isn't nailed down or unbreakable. They particularly like to squeeze all of the bras hanging on display. Like a cat, a toddler will want to get in and out of the cart every twenty seconds or so. You have to decide when to stop this game and then listen to the screaming.

Children will want to purchase everything they see. The trick is (only works under the age of four or so) to agree to purchase it, and if they're still looking, place it in your cart. Then take it out of the cart five minutes later. Put it on another shelf. That's why you see miniature cars haphazardly placed on top of stainless steel frying pans. They won't notice, because they'll be busy eyeballing the next item. If the item is something you know you will eventually use (for a while my daughter insisted on buying glue every time we went out), buy it anyway and store it for the future. Use your "no"s sparingly. They have to learn that things are either too expensive or unnecessary. You can tell them this at home if they discover their coveted item hasn't made it back. They can have their tantrum in your house instead of in the store. Another favorite trick of Supermoms is to tell them that you would buy it, but will you look at that, it doesn't come in their size. Works pretty well.

Three-year-olds will not understand why the store insists on putting all those items on display if they can't have any of it. They suppose some nice mom somewhere is picking up these treasures for her lucky children.

Life is full of things we can look at but can't touch. Stacks of twenty-dollar bills at the bank, greasy fried foods when we're on a diet, Brad Pitt...you get the idea. A good lesson for your children to learn early. Of course you're dealing with an audience here who thinks each color of Smarties tastes different, and that the Rugrats-shaped pasta noodles taste different than the regular macaroni noodles. She won't be into absorbing life's lessons when all she wants is the mega-sized peanut butter cups.

With older kids, you can tell them "yes," as long as *they* are willing to pay for it. Make them understand the value of their purchase by comparing it to other items they may want. You will still get the "it's not fair" remark, but they too need to understand the value of money. Don't ever give them an advance on their allowance—they're usually not good for it. "Don't ask for credit as refusal may offend," as the old saying goes.

Grocery shopping is a whole other adventure. Find a store with live fish or lobsters, and you have something akin to visiting the pet store at the mall. Save it for the end of the trip, so you can wave it like a carrot for the shopping period. You cannot browse with young children, so make sure you have prepared a detailed list, by section. Older children can be sent on missions to gather some of the items, which they enjoy doing.

Whenever possible, don't take your children shopping—it's almost always a miserable experience for both of you. When you have to, make it short and sweet and reward yourself if you can get home without yelling at them once. Okay, twice.

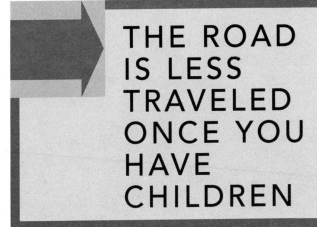

THE ROAD IS LESS TRAVELED ONCE YOU HAVE CHILDREN

Sure, Supermom goes on vacation. With. Her. Kids. Remember idyllic holidays where you could relax and enjoy yourself? Holidays where you don't go to "find yourself," but rather to "lose yourself"? Long morning sleep-ins, late lunches, early cocktails, late cocktails, pointless chatter, meaningless relationships? It goes straight to hell once you have children. If you don't have the organization of a sergeant major, the possibility of having even ten minutes of enjoyable time on a family holiday is unlikely. Traveling with children—via car, plane, train, or boat—will be a harrowing, stressful experience. Take the usual advice of drugging your children before any long trips, and accept that "holiday" is a relative term. Many Supermoms convince themselves that their children *do* have motion sickness so they can justify shoving double dosages of Dramamine down their throats. They're very aware of that little side effect that knocks children unconscious for several hours.

The benefit of traveling in your own car, while still a confined space, is that fellow road travelers cannot hear the screams and rants constantly emanating from your vehicle. Unless they try really hard. Short of having the allowance of Paris Hilton, however, if you travel by airplane you will be surrounded by either "innocent bystanders," or "interfering busybodies," depending on your mood. An airplane journey can be a great experience with a very young infant. It's an entirely different story traveling with any other age child, particularly before the age of ten. Toddlers running about on planes and screaming at the top of their lungs is not a good time for anyone. The infant stage is great because not only does the tiniest drop of Tylenol (I'd swear he was a bit feverish too) leave him groggy, but airline personnel are likely to offer to take Junior for a little walk should he be getting a bit fussy. It's perfect—they can't abduct the baby so you can relax and let them take over.

Don't make the amateur's mistake of walking the child up and down the aisles yourself. This is another of the "don't do once what you don't want to do 100 times" items.

Over the age of three, bribery is your best weapon in dealing with children on extensive journeys. For long car trips, purchase small items from the dollar store as rewards for a quiet hour. The hour starts over every time there is an altercation or generally bad behavior. If your trip is scheduled for six hours, and you have four small children in the car, you won't need twenty-four gifts. Running out of treats is not an option, so come prepared or know how to set the car clock back. Wet wipes, tissues, grocery bags, and pens and paper will always come in handy. They're not bribes, but necessary tools of survival if you want to arrive sane.

The best way to get through a holiday with your kids is to go somewhere truly kid-friendly. Slapping a "Kids Club" logo on a few empty storage rooms does not a fun experience make. A bored child is a miserable child, and you will be the recipient of this misery. The best family vacations are the ones where you don't have to spend too much time with your own family.

Try to remember that family time is important, even when they're driving you crazy. It's a perfect opportunity to trap your children into talking to you, or even tricking them into singing songs a la Brady Bunch. When you get to your home away from home, always look for a hotel that has a liquor license and room service. You'll need it to feel like *you're* getting away from it all too.

PART 6:

First Time
Supermoms—
You're Not Being
Paranoid, We *Are*
Laughing at You

"Parents were invented to make children happy by giving them something to ignore."

—Ogden Nash

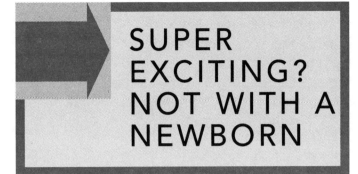

SUPER EXCITING? NOT WITH A NEWBORN

The time spent with a newborn provides you with the most challenging and the most boring times of your Supermom life. This is particularly true when the newborn is your first child, and besides dealing with the overwhelming new responsibilities, you're also dealing with your own neuroses.

Should he sleep on his back? Front? Side? The safest position for preventing Sudden Infant Death Syndrome seems to change every few years. Should you breast-feed or bottle-feed? To vaccinate or not to vaccinate? To go to them when they wake up or let them cry? To feed them on demand or on a schedule? To cut back their food if they're getting too fat? The list of concerns with newborns grows exponentially each day after they're born.

So baby is asleep. Now what? So many exciting tasks to choose from: laundry, bottles, putting cream on cracked nipples, a shower, a quick vacuum. What happened to reading through emails, gossiping about the weird techie guys and sneaking down for a coffee? Ah, the good old days. Any task is impossible if you keep running back to the crib every three minutes to make sure that baby is breathing normally. The baby will undoubtedly wake up at the precise moment you've started to relax. The Supermom philosophy should be to engage in certain tasks only when baby is awake. For example, loading/unloading dishwashers, laundry, vacuuming, and putting away groceries can all be done with a baby in the room. Reading a book or taking a quiet bath cannot. For the record, drinking wine can be done anytime. Choose your activities carefully and be realistic about what you can get done by the end of the day. Sometimes a shower is a great accomplishment. Just wait until you have to go back to work. This time will seem like a breeze.

We've all seen the sappy movies and advertisements with the parents gazing adoringly at their new babies as though they could watch them all night. Truthfully, watching a newborn move their fingers, squint their eyes, and curl their toes can only entertain even the most doting parents or grandparents for a maximum of six-and-a-half minutes. After that, come on, the paint drying in their nursery was better than this.

Infants aren't terribly interactive; they can't go anywhere, and they have very basic needs. When babies start to play with blocks, pots and pans, and anything else they can get their chubby hands on is when it really becomes an exercise in brain strain. Forget building great towers out of blocks for baby to enjoy—you'll be lucky to get two stacked up before they knock them down. Forget sitting happily in one place and playing. The minute you have all their toys set up in a tidy semicircle around them, they will either barf, whack themselves on the head with a toy, fall over, crawl away, or take a big dump. Their time management skills are extremely poor.

Once your child enters the world under your guard, your life ceases to be your own. You won't resent it, but you'd better get used to it quickly. Once you've given this gift (not of life itself, but of *your* life) to the child, what could it hurt to have one or two more?

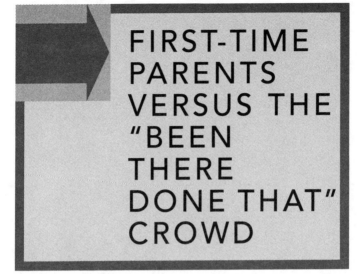

FIRST-TIME PARENTS VERSUS THE "BEEN THERE DONE THAT" CROWD

Supermoms become quickly adept at picking out first time parents (amateurs!). Here are some identifying marks of the first-time parent:

1) Arranges entire social schedule around baby's nap time and feeding time, while still believing they can carry on with the same level of productivity at work and at home.

2) Bathes baby daily, with special infant tub, special infant washcloths, and special infant soap. Baby is then lovingly wrapped in special baby hooded towel.

3) Brand spanking new turbo stroller, with nary a vomit stain or mud splat in sight. Bottom basket neatly organized and cleaned daily.

4) Baby infant car seat seen to be in pristine condition and perfect working order, straps set at precisely the right distances.

5) Homemade baby food. Say no more.

The more seasoned parenting crowd (i.e. those with more than one precious bundle):

1) Baby naps whenever/wherever they can. Parents are generally unaware when last nap took place and how long it might have been. As long as baby is sleeping through the night, this is not important.

2) Baby is bathed when cheesy neck is detected, same baby food carrot stain has been noted by relatives for more than one week, and baby is generally crusty. Baths can take place in the bathroom sink, lying down in the real bathtub with an inch of water, or baby is stuffed into plastic laundry basket for easy propping. Any towel will do, and who needs a washcloth when your hands feel so much nicer.

3) Stroller emits volumes of crumbs, dried-out wet wipes, and half-sucked, dribbling juice boxes each time it is folded or unfolded. Straps are

twisted and the plastic ends are generally cracked or broken, which isn't a problem because the baby is seldom strapped in. The difference between the time they *need* strapping in and the time that they figure out how to wriggle out of the strap is approximately twenty minutes. Bottom basket is generally a sticky, dirty mess. Don't go there.

4) The baby's car seat features baby food remnants and spit-up stains, and its twisted straps never seem to be long enough for the growing baby. Tendency to force the issue, resulting in a strange, hunchbacked look for Junior. Their young bodies are quite flexible, so not to worry.

5) Jarred baby food is used from six to nine months, generally, after which time baby is relegated to a regular diet of table scraps, cut up or mushed into a pulp. They're fine.

While all of the above is usually true, the one surefire way to detect a first time parent is to ask them how old their child is. If they know within the week for a child under one year of age, or within the month for a child over two—i.e. thirty nine months old—you have yourself a virgin to these parts.

THE DIAPER BAG—A TREASURE TROVE OF CRAP

Just as a Supermom may have to trade in her sports car for a minivan (gasp), your ultra sleek leather briefcase is about to morph into a dreaded diaper bag, or a "baby convenience carryall." The only people who carry diaper bags (real, true diaper bags with the Beatrix Potter designs) are first-time Moms. They are brainwashed into believing they need all of the little sections and paraphernalia (e.g. change pad) that come with it. Check any inexperienced Mom's diaper bag and you will find:

* At least three additional outfits even when the baby normally only goes through that many changes in that many days;
* Six to eight diapers, ranging in size, just in case of a sudden growth spurt;

* The aforementioned change pad, which conveniently folds over to the approximate size of a foam pillow (hint: babies don't need the lumbar support);
* Two to three bottles plus a can or two of ready-to-serve formula, even if they're breast-fed (Mom may be mowed down in an accident, Junior is starving, and innocent passersby may have to search the bag for emergency food);
* An emergency pacifier, potentially pre-sterilized and placed with sterilized tongs inside a sterile, ziplocked plastic bag;
* Two to three plastic bags for handy poopy diaper storage—often returned home, filled with the poopy diaper. You wouldn't want to throw away baby's sewage just anywhere;
* Four to six bibs, particularly if baby is eating solids. "Days of the week" bibs are sorted chronologically and intended for use on their prescribed day;
* A new bottle of baby Tylenol "just in case";
* Plastic wipes container, full to the brim with the expensive, pre-packaged wipes (not the bulk, no brand-name type);
* Two to three receiving blankets, freshly laundered, still laboriously used over the

shoulder by Mom until she realizes babies can aim what they spew. Babies believe that the game is called "keep the blanket clean";

* Zinc-based diaper cream.

Mom will likely have her own purse in tow, as she will still be laboring under the delusion that she is her own person and has her own life.

In contrast, the experienced Supermom will have the following:

* Her own carryall bag, black to hide stains;
* One diaper (you can buy them anywhere, after all), the right size, or near enough;
* One pre-filled bottle of formula (it's good up to six or eight hours, isn't it?);
* A couple of wipes in a plastic bag, the bag opened to allow cracker crumbs to nestle inside the wipes themselves;
* A baby t-shirt, maybe (once used it is never replaced);
* Her wallet.

That's it. The bib is on the baby (remember, babies are pigs and require constant mopping up), the pacifier is attached with a handy pacifier leash, the clothes we'll make do with, and forget the Tylenol, as fevers/aches/pains only happen at 2:00 in the morning when you have an important meeting the next day. The receiving blanket is usually stuffed into the baby's lap already, with all noticeable stains turned downwards. Forget the change pad; the stinky blanket will suffice. Forget the diaper cream too, as, again, diaper rash only hits in the middle of the night or during an elaborate dinner party. Mothers will note that I have left out all of the disgusting crud found in diaper bags belonging to those with older children. Used tissues, little toy cars, at least two crappy McDonald's toys, a licked lollipop without the wrapper, a half-eaten apple, broken crayons, etc., abound.

Unless you are leaving the country for parts unknown, the "emergency" supplies are simply not required. Every drugstore sells formula and bottles and pacifiers and diapers, and you can't go far in the civilized world without tripping over a drugstore. Necessity is the mother of invention, after all. You'd be surprised what amazing baby items you can turn a table napkin into, if the situation demands it. Go easy on yourself and your back, and only carry the minimum. Every mother knows you can't go shopping without buying at least one little thing for the baby, at any rate. Try to resist that second "really cute" diaper bag.

PART 7:

Building Your Child's Independence through Basic Lack of Interest and Time

"Nothing has a stronger influence psychologically on their environment and especially on their children than the unlived life of the parent."

—Carl Jung

LESSONS, BLOODY LESSONS

Supermoms are well aware of the wide assortment of lessons available to give their children a head start in life. They are even more aware of the fact that there are 24 hours in each day. From swimming to skating to karate to jazz dance, you have to have your child in some sort of lesson. If you don't, you are just...well, a bad parent. You will have absolutely nothing to talk about with your friends, family, and even casual acquaintances. Good advice for Supermoms is to continually switch your children's lessons so that they don't get too good at any one thing and want to start to compete or practice more than once a week. This isn't cruel; it's the "Jack of all trades, Master of none" strategy. This will make your children well-rounded, flexible, and appreciative of the interests of others. *Yeah, right.* It also keeps you from having to sit in a hockey arena five times a week after getting up out of a warm bed at 5:00 a.m. to drive halfway across town. Even Canadian Supermoms don't get the hockey thing. Understanding what men like about it—the hitting, the swearing, the jocularity (and that's all in the locker room prior to the game) is easy, but the Hockey Mom thing is something else.

The Hockey Mom is a very distant relation of the Soccer Mom. Very distant. A curious breed. Their goal is not clear. Perhaps the NHL, perhaps goal-scoring bragging rights, and perhaps just the pleasure of seeing their sons or daughters compete and excel. It can't be the company in the stands. Brutal. The obsessed Homer is in her element here: she has a captive audience for at least an hour at a stretch. The talk may start off about hockey and the game being watched, but it quickly degenerates to a rag session about the coach, the other parents, the other kids, the Supermoms who never come to watch the games, and anyone else who dares to cross her path.

The hours some Homers can put into their children's extracurricular activities is astonishing. If your child is truly talented and driven—in the opinion of others, not just you—this is one thing. If you're doing this for yourself, please stop. Competitiveness can be good, but winning shouldn't be your child's sole motivation. There are far more losers in the world than winners, and I mean that in the nicest way. For every winning goal scored and for every first place ribbon, there are many more children lined up behind who worked just as hard and sacrificed just as much free time to get there. My only hope is that they all had an equal amount of fun.

This type of abhorrent maternal behavior is not limited to hockey. It manifests itself slightly differently with each sport. You hear a lot about Soccer Moms, but I believe that term is really a euphemism about a certain lifestyle—the lifestyle of the van driving, pedicured, pampered, and slightly airheady Stay-At-Home Mom. Even the swimming pool, where important lifesaving skills are taught, is not safe. There are Swim Moms. These are the women who will yell across the pool to their youngsters in their quest to assist the fully qualified instructors. Teach them yourself if you don't trust the professionals.

Sign your children up for classes you think they will enjoy. If you really want them to take a particular class, don't ask them if they want to go. Supermoms just sign them up and take them. Young children aren't normally aware of where they are going at any rate. If they beg you to sign them up for a class you normally wouldn't want them in ("Acting for Television Commercials" springs to mind) and the price is reasonable, let them do it, with the caveat that they are not allowed to drop out until the term is over. Also, limit the amount of time this "scheduled play" takes. Kids need to learn how to amuse themselves outside of a formal setting. They may accidentally discover some other new talents in free play as well.

SUPERMOMS HAVE SUPERGROUPS

Some Supermoms have been known to quit corporate life and retire to the homestead. Fairly quickly they throw themselves into organizing something...anything to flex and share their now untapped professional skills. One of the scariest examples of this flexing is in the plethora of "moms groups" that have sprung up with alarming frequency in the last five years or so. Ex-Supermoms cannot settle for casual "coffee klatches" with friends like our mothers did. Many Homers will kindly open their doors to the ex-Supermoms who have given up their "little jobs" outside the home, and before they know it, the enemy has taken over. These ubergroups are more organized, more professional, more "in tune with our children's needs and those of our own as women." Yikes. Mothers now arrange "play dates" (I swear I'll slap the next person who uses that terminology), rather than getting together for a gossip and a fattening assortment of cookies and cakes. It has given way to "drop in" mornings at the local indoor playground, "playground meetings" at a certain time and place in a particular park, with attendees assigned a consumable to bring for "the girls."

Some moms groups have gotten Superorganized and have newsletters, flyers, bake sales, family days, BBQ picnics...in aid of what exactly is not clear. Exciting articles that appear in the newsletter might include:

* *The Family Bed: Heaven or Hell?*
* *Bottles at Three Years Old—Let the Child Decide*
* *Forcing Your Friends (and Strangers) to Breastfeed*
* *101 Ways to Avoid Sex, a Good Haircut, and Shaving Your Legs*
* *How Does Your Newborn Measure Up? Twenty Telltale Signs You're in Trouble*

Makes a self-respecting active Supermom shudder. But with all of these purposeful women attending these well organized events and meetings, at the bottom of it all, the sole purpose hasn't changed all that much. It's to swap war stories (i.e. childbirth and husbands), garner support in the hard times, and celebrate the good times. Maybe even share a chuckle at the expense of another, once in a while. Perhaps we have traded in the homemade coffee and banana bread for Starbucks Dark Roast and biscotti, but the main objectives of trading interesting and useful child-raising tips and ripping other women apart hasn't changed.

Each moms group is like a mini-society, and they are fairly protective of their inner circle and mildly disdainful of lookalike groups they see. They certainly don't like the women they can't convince to join them. It's like an Amway sales drive. They try to make you feel morally inept and lazy if you opt out. A lot of the most zealous women in these groups have given up a fairly good career in order to devote themselves to their children. They *need* to feel needed, they *need* someone to boss around, and most of all they *need* to boost their own self-confidence by tearing down someone else. As a Supermom, give them some fodder for their upcoming meetings the next time you run across them in an indoor playground or a Starbucks. Feed your children chocolate bars for lunch. Give them Diet Pepsi as a chaser. Yell at them to not worry about washing their hands after a number two, as they'll just get their hands dirty again on the play equipment. If you can, blurt out a swear word in front of the kids and then tell them it's only because you have a massive hangover that you're acting this way. You'll have given these women many hours of pleasure and self-confidence. Think of it as an act of charity.

It would be wrong to give the impression that all women's groups are cesspools of gossip and backstabbing. That's more like the office. There are some out there, though. Choose carefully and align yourself with people who make you feel good about being connected, not inferior or mean-spirited when the session is over. As my children used to say, "If you can't say anything nice...then shut up!"

CHILDREN'S TELEVISION— SAVIOR OR SATAN?

Supermoms have a love/hate relationship with children's television. We absolutely adore it at 5:30 in the evening, when we're trying to get dinner ready, the baby is finally asleep in his swing, and the three older children can find a show they will all watch together. We hate television when they are fighting over the remote control, it is turned up too loud, or worst of all it becomes their most interesting hobby. And they let the Homers in the neighborhood in on that fact.

At their core, children's shows are nothing more than a half-hour, or sometimes a torturous hour-long, commercial for a product. The worst offender was the rash of Pokemon/Digimon/Yu-Gi-Oh/Bey-Blades specifically targeted at a very vulnerable group: six- to twelve-year-old boys. Traditionally this group has been largely ignored. Sure, they've had their G.I. Joes, their Tonka toys, and their Erector sets (all of these toys have been around for more than thirty years), but they didn't ever get into the Cabbage Patch craze, the Tickle Me Elmo fanaticism, or the longstanding love affair with Barbie. Each Pokemon, et al., series targeted to these boys involves approximately 150-200 characters, each of which *must* be purchased in card format, or recently, a more expensive plastic disk. Ten-year-old boys do not know what day of the week it is most of the time, but they can reel off the names of these characters, their super powers, their evolved form, and the names of all of their relatives with no problem at all.

Remember Pac-Man? Asteroids? Nothing but a small table-like screen at your local café or bar. There was no association with t-shirts, trading cards, rulers, backpacks, or any of the assorted merchandise we see today. And they call the '80s the "Material Age." Were we more individual? Perhaps. Although I do remember that we had to have acid-washed jeans, high-top sneakers, and a Members Only jacket to be considered cool.

It's pointless trying to keep your children entirely away from television. At best, they can learn a lot from it. And I don't mean restricting them to the History Channel or PBS. Television can get them involved in the social issues and trends of the day. They need to be familiar with these programs in order to fit into the playground. They don't have to purchase every single item that accessorizes these shows, but a basic knowledge keeps them out of the geek category.

Some Moms severely limit the television their children watch. The problem is when they visit a family without these restrictions, they will sit absolutely transfixed to the set, ignoring the pool, ping pong table, and other recreational games which might be available. I suppose it gives their parents the ability to visit without interruption, but I believe their kids will eventually become more obsessed with the forbidden TV than those children who are allowed to select the times when they want to indulge.

It's important to monitor what your children watch. Even cartoons can teach racism, violence, and wicked stereotypes. Make sure you watch at least one episode of your child's favorite show. Some of the shows aimed at young adults are the favorites of our 'tweens, so be watchful of the information they're receiving about drugs, sex, and other fun topics.

Encourage your children to find a show that you can all watch together as a family. It can't be a typical "kids" show if you want to get through it too without feeling as though your ears are bleeding. There are many science shows that hold great fascination for children. There are specials on the circus, ballet, plays, etc., that you think they may not like, but you'll be pleasantly surprised when they do.

Television has been called the "electronic babysitter"— not always a negative. Until you've attempted to make dinner, do laundry, listen to voice mail, watch a toddler, correct homework, and sweep up broken glass all at the same time (that is, within the first hour you get home from work), you're not really in a position to judge television as a lifesaver for an overworked parent (a redundant term). The Others are often known to sniff that if they had children they suppose that once in a while they would "allow the television to baby-sit if they were feeling lazy." Once you get over the overwhelming urge to slap them, you realize that this is just another aspect of having children that you cannot explain to the childless. And those who claim, "I have nieces and nephews, I know what it's like," are full of crap. Having a niece or nephew around for a few hours versus raising your own children is like comparing a stubbed toe to a total lower body amputation.

Television is a part of our culture, like it or not. So, just like you wouldn't dress your ten-year-old daughter in frilly pioneer dresses in the year 2005, you'd better accept that the socialization that comes from watching television is part of our children's landscape. Just don't hurt yourself trying to understand what *SpongeBob SquarePants* is really all about.

IT'S THEIR HOMEWORK, NOT YOURS

Supermoms barely register what their child's teacher's name is, let alone have a working knowledge of their homework schedule and demands. Homers, on the other hand, like to take on their child's homework, particularly when there is a project involved. Supermom doesn't have enough minutes in the day to get this involved. Not all future professions require terrific grades in building pyramids out of household objects. Children should try to complete their own homework and, occasionally, they will falter. It's the journey that's important, not the destination. They'll at least be appropriately graded to see what their true strengths and weaknesses really are.

The Homers who devote themselves to their child's success at such an early stage are everywhere, from the public school system to the most exclusive private schools. It's not uncommon to overhear two otherwise normal women talking about a project they are working on for their children, and having trouble getting it done because they are falling behind in the tutoring work. The child gets sent to the tutor because they're not getting good grades. They don't get good grades because Homer is doing all of the work for them. They don't do well with the tutor, either. Homer ends up doing the work there, too, so that the tutor won't think the child isn't working, or—dare we say it—smart enough. Go figure.

There are parents who spend hours on their children's school projects to get them looking just perfect. Homers are often seen at ungodly hours ferrying art projects (entire buildings built out of cardboard) to school. These parents are obsessed with that elusive "A" for fourth grade art. Supermoms shouldn't be surprised to find a good number of teachers who are either unwilling or uninterested in giving these "overhelped" children bad grades even when it's apparent that they've had help. Few teachers will give the highest marks to the projects that definitely are not the most professional looking, where it's painfully obvious the children have done the work themselves. Supermom conspiracy theories would speculate that the

Homering commitment to the school activities contributes to the blind eye grading.

The parents who believe they are doing their children a great service by protecting them in this manner are more likely teaching them that they don't have ultimate responsibility for their own work. This is fine for children who aspire to work in the government or banking sectors. Otherwise it can be a problem. These children may have difficulty when they get to high school, college, or grad school, and realize they are expected to do 100 percent of the work and no one will be nagging them to do it. Well, maybe that annoying Senior Vice President, but other than him.

Don't spell check everything your kids do—they'll learn from their mistakes. Don't insist they use the computer for graphics unless they have been specifically asked to do so—let them use their imaginations and put pencil to paper. They will not develop self-confidence if they haven't accomplished anything entirely on their own. Learning to fail is just as important as being successful, otherwise how will they know the difference?

PART 8:

Enrolled in a
Parenting
Class? Loser.

"The thing that impresses me the most about America is the way parents obey their children."

—King Edward VIII

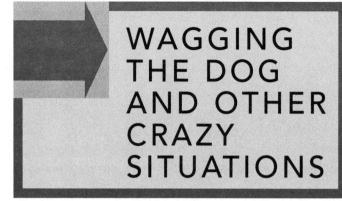

WAGGING THE DOG AND OTHER CRAZY SITUATIONS

Supermoms are totally in control at work. At least most of the time, and when it really matters. There is a delicate balance of power that is respected in the traditional chain of command in a business environment. This balance is rarely tipped. For example, junior product managers do not determine the long-term strategy for anything more important than a new coffee machine for the floor. Yet inside some homes, a strange occurrence is taking place. Junior is in control. Supermoms may well ask themselves, "Who's in charge here?" This is a question that, in fact, reverberates around many people's heads when they watch the absolute control some children seem to have over their parents. This goes against nature, surely. Yet it is a phenomenon that seems to have afflicted the current parenting generation like no other before it. It is continuously astounding the way in which these little Nazis (little *Precious* to their parents) yell, shriek, and torture their parents into getting exactly what they want, each time. Bedtime at 11:00 for a four-year-old? Sure. Candies and chips before dinner? Why not. A new pair of shoes they don't need and won't look at ten minutes after purchase? Naturally. I think the reason these folks scare Supermoms so much is that we are afraid we will turn into them if we let our guard down for just one minute with the little bastards. There's a realization of "Hey, hold on, I didn't want to do that," that comes over us when we find ourselves being expertly manipulated by two-year-old tears or eleven-year-old tirades.

Good luck to 'em is all I can say. If the child has the ability to control their lives from infancy, they are in for a rough ride when puberty hits. Some basic rules to help keep your children from ruling the roost:

Don't ask the question if you don't want the wrong answer. If there is no choice, tell them what to do. Administrative assistants are not asked if they would like to prepare your monthly expense report or not, neither should toddlers be asked if they would like to wear mittens before going ice skating. This is the time for issuing orders, not seeking opinions. Supermoms learn to never, never, never ask a child a question unless they are prepared to consider alternative options. "Do you want to go to bed now?" "Are you going to finish your broccoli?" "Do you want your face to stay like that?" These are questions to which there is only one answer and you don't want to hear it. Toddlers do not understand the concept of the rhetorical question. Fighting over a plate of steamed vegetables in a public restaurant is not the place to start teaching them.

With the exception of allergies and religious beliefs, *do not make substitutions at meal times.* While it can be tempting both from a time and money perspective to let your child have peanut butter sandwiches for breakfast, lunch, and dinner every day, it doesn't teach the social grace of eating whatever crap is put in front of you. This is a skill which serves us all well when dining at in-laws' houses.

Wake them from their nap if you have plans—particularly if being late will disrupt the plans of others. You show up on time for work (mostly), so don't keep other time-pressed parents waiting because you suffer from "nappus interupptus avoidance."

Little Precious is having her nap and you can't leave the house until she wakes up? Sadly, this is not an uncommon scenario. "Adult" plans all over town are being disrupted due to the parents' inability to take control of their lives. Parents like this refuse to take control of their child and at the same time provide flexibility training for their children.

Stop treating them like babies if they're not babies. If you are still preparing mashed up baby food when the "baby" is close to entering preschool, stop. Please. Stop catering to their every need. Respectable Supermom children are likely to be found gnawing their way through a T-bone steak or beef curry at age two. Bottles are not for toddlers. They are for baby formula and wine. If your child is playing Game Boy while you change his diaper, it is time to start toilet training. If he has to take his pacifier out of his mouth to advise you how he would like his steak done at a restaurant, it is time to cut the nipple. Of the pacifier.

Throw out clothes you don't want them to wear (in this case the "them" refers to husbands as well). A four-year-old would wear the same Spiderman T-shirt every day until the dried-up ketchup on it begins to scratch her skin. A nine-year-old would *live* in sweatpants if you let him, which to a Supermom is the ultimate slob wear. Hide his one pair of sweatpants and put them in his knapsack for gym day only. Otherwise he will wear them to your office Christmas party. Clothes have a way of mysteriously disappearing in my house—including my husband's blue denim plaid shirt.

Don't offer an explanation for everything. "I'm your mother and I said so," is acceptable and common Supermomspeak. Marketing Vice Presidents don't explain why the bank needs to change its 150 year old logo at a huge expense; it's just "the strategy." Likewise, no Supermom should be caught explaining why it is wrong to stick your friends with a fork.

Don't do anything once that you do not want to repeat 100 times. "Okay, but just this once," is translated into the following for young children: "Okay, you win, we will always do everything you want to do even if I have argued with you about it for an hour." This Supermom will never forgive her sister for allowing my then two-year-old son to wear his sister's dress to the park "just this once" that day. Neither will he, thanks to the wonder of photography.

Establish a schedule for fast food dining. Once a week might be a good benchmark to aim for. If the children know that Friday night is fast food night, they won't be begging for it every other night of the week. In a Supermom house, fast food night is the one night the children eat *good* food, rather than crap you make them. Even if you don't set out to use fast food as a reward, they will see it as one. Something about unwrapping food from paper packages. Supermoms get the same feeling about food that is served to them—doesn't have to be good, you just want someone else to bring it to you for a change.

Self-fulfilling prophecies work. If you don't *expect* your children to sleep through the night until they are five years old, they won't. If you *expect* they can behave in a grocery store, they just may. State your expectations to them; if they hear it often enough they could surprise you. However, no one is optimistic or naïve enough to suggest that this is the answer to all behavioral problems. Many times Supermom can be heard telling her children about their expectations for good behavior, no swearing, no spitting, etc., only to have them interpret the list as activity suggestions. What it does do, however, is set up the punishment if the rules are broken. Did you tell them you expected no shoving in the grocery store and no name-calling in the swimming pool? If they proceed to do it, then you should be able to dole out the punishments without much whining about "I didn't know we weren't allowed to do *that.*"

Try to appear as though you are in control. While this sounds obvious, think to yourself, "Am I acting in a manner which indicates I am the one in control?" Screeching at a two-year-old to "grow up and get it together" is usually an indication that this is not true.

You can easily catch an older brother talking his younger sister into performing physically dangerous tasks (skateboards and winding stairs come to mind), and his defense will likely be, "But she likes it. She wants to do it." To which any Supermom is happy to produce the standard parent reply, "She's four. She doesn't know any better." Now if this is true about activities that can cause bodily harm, it is almost certainly true about most other ill-advised decisions as well. Children are not the best resource for logic and long term implications. When all else fails, ask yourself "Would Mike Brady let them get away with this? And if they did it anyway, would I have to come up with one of those confusing 'Well, if we do bad things to other people and bad things happen to us as a result of the bad things we did' speeches that were his specialty?" If so, I think you have your answer. Kids are human, and the "give 'em an inch and they'll take a mile" rule was written with them in mind.

STEP ASIDE AND LET THE PROFESSIONALS TAKE OVER

Capitalizing on Supermom guilt is a cottage industry. The latest trend is *parenting coaches*. It's exactly what you think. Apparently between our parents' generation and ours, on the way to achieving equal rights and earning respectable salaries, all the common sense normally attributed to Mom has been lost. Now a personal guide is mandatory for becoming a good parent. And these "professional" coaches are just the people to show Supermom the way. It was probably inevitable. The parenting seminar route is now well-traveled, and, like the aerobics classes that have evolved to personal trainers, now Supermoms need a little one-on-one to ensure that they maximize their offspring's potential in every way possible.

By mistake, you may have found yourself at a parenting seminar. The lecturer will normally be quite out of touch with reality and you will wonder how she has managed to get herself dressed and out the door that morning. You may hear a parenting theory that states that bribery is an inappropriate tool for getting children to behave. Huh? Supermom doesn't get this. Isn't our whole capitalist society built on rewarding those who do a good job? A new position, a promotion, a raise, a gold star, a good grade, a happy marriage, etc. What better time to learn these principles than when you're a child.

You may hear attacks on one of the mainstays of parental bribery: The Allowance. A "parenting expert" would state that allowance should not be tied to any particular chore or behavior around the house, but rather be a sort of "good will" gesture by virtue of being part of the family. If the child desires to clean her room anyway (I hear you laughing), she will then be motivated to do it for the satisfaction of being a contributing member of the family. And these experts are normally drug-free. They're also normally child-free as well, or they're full of crap. Supermom knows that the only way to get any work done around the house with children is either through the reward or punishment system.

"Clean up your room or there's no TV for a
week."

"Take out the garbage and I'll give you fifty cents."

"Fish the dead chipmunk out of the pool and I'll give you ten dollars."

Even Supermoms are human, and while there are some things we do for the intrinsic good (helping an old lady across the street, for example), most things we do benefit us personally in some way, either long term or short term. For goodness sake, even charitable donations are tax deductible. Poo in the toilet, get a Smartie. It's all the same thing.

The same parenting wingnut who doesn't believe in the reward system won't believe in giving children false praise. This can be a good thing. Nothing makes Supermoms more sick than a parent saying "good girl" to a child who is clearly not behaving. They could have one valid point. Stop listening, though, or you'll find out that that this applies to things such as their artwork as well. "No three-year-old," they will explain, "can produce a good painting or picture, so we should not insist on telling them that they are good. They will believe that they will grow up to be an artist, when clearly they are not talented." What planet are these people from? Any decent parent knows that saying, "What a great picture" to a toddler is not an expression of how good the actual painting is, but of the creative process and concentration (hey, they sat still for thirty seconds) that went into it. No, it's not good art, but praise gives them the self-confidence to continue to try new things.

The best parenting seminar you will ever attend or parenting coach you will ever need can be found by going out to dinner with three or four of your closest friends who have children, and learning from each other. Experience is the best teacher in this particular field.

THE PET THING

No self-respecting Supermom should ever take on a pet. You have enough crap to clean up (at work and at home), and your time demands are already overloaded without adding this fresh hell. Most Supermoms are not pet people. Many may be pretending to be a pet person for the sake of their families. Homers in the suburbs can't live without a pet.

Any kind of pet is too much work. A dog, cat, bird, turtle, fish, ferret, snake, hamster, guinea pig, mouse, rat—there seems to be a new kind added every year. Never mind a pot-bellied pig. It's not as though your children wouldn't love a pet. They would—preferably a large dog. As a Supermom, it's hard to justify another dependent, non-toilet-trained, messy-eating, disobedient character in the house.

Try to convince your children that fish are the ultimate fun in pets if you have to take this route.

They'll see how much work a pet can be if you make them clean out the aquarium on a regular basis. Try to get a particular breed of incontinent goldfish if you can. The tank will be disgusting in no time. It will get so cloudy that the kids can make a game out of seeing if they can spot their fish. With any luck, one day, through the murky water, you will notice two golden bellies floating on the top. How to explain this disheartening turn of events? Even if you've only had the fish for a couple of months, you fear they might be heartbroken. Sit the kids down and tell them that you have some very bad news. Tell them straight out that their fish are no longer among the living. Any child under five is likely to look you straight in the eye and say, "Oh well, I didn't like them anyway. Can I have a snack?" You can live off the "I let you have a pet once and look what happened" line for quite a while.

We've all heard the jokes about who the master is and who the slave is, but it is no more obvious than with a dog. You see them everywhere: men, women, and (rarely) children marching along on a dark, rainy morning, plastic grocery bag firmly in hand, ready to scoop up a nice warm pile of crap when his majesty finally deigns to release some of his bounty. Call me crazy, but it's not a lifestyle any

Supermom needs to aspire to. A dog is a make-work project gone haywire.

Many of the people who have dogs feel that there would be something missing in their lives without one. A Supermom doesn't have any time to be missing anything. Dogs provide a handy excuse for being needed. Supermoms are already needed by too many people. Once personal needs are met by a new job, a new baby, a new or rekindled relationship, you may no longer feel the need for the dog and you may become resentful of the dog's neediness. Some people treat their dogs with more love and respect than their own families (some understandably so). However, Supermom needs to spend more time pouring that love and support (and hard work, frankly) into her children, her marriage, and her job.

Many Others use their pets as a substitute for children, although they would never admit it. Even the most adamantly childless couples put themselves at the beck and call of their dogs, without for a minute recognizing the irony of the situation. A dog isn't going to visit you in your old age (they'll die first), or provide you with countless moments of pride and admiration. Admittedly some children won't either, but they all clean up their own poo after the age of five.

Before you decide to take on a pet, know this, Supermom—YOU will be the sole and primary caregiver for this pet. If you are prepared to take this on, great. If you're not, see if you can borrow a neighbor's dog for the kids to walk (without being paid, of course), complete with pooper scooping responsibility. I think the appeal will soon wear off. If it doesn't, perhaps your child is that one in a million who will truly look after their own pet. Most children can't keep track of a pair of gym shoes for longer than a day or two, so you probably won't be planning a trip down to PetSmart anytime soon.

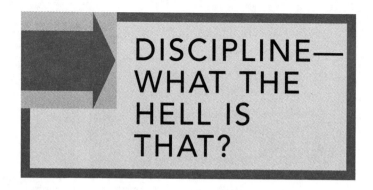

DISCIPLINE—WHAT THE HELL IS THAT?

Need to fire someone? Give a new, enthusiastic employee a harsh review? Berate a supplier? Child's play compared to trying to understand the politically correct and effective methods for disciplining children. Supermoms are confused. What works better, the humane way of talking to your children, giving time-outs, and grounding, or the cruel way of spanking (gasp!), shouting, and verbal abuse? What's a Supermom to do?

The type of discipline you employ will largely depend on the child. Each of them can be disciplined slightly differently in order to achieve maximum impact. Basically it is ideal if they learn from their "mistakes," and have some remorse. Don't buy into the theory that "there are no bad children, just bad behavior." There are bad kids. Jeffrey Dahmer was a kid once. The child that grows up with this philosophy may become the adult who will take no responsibility for their actions (i.e. suing a bar for letting them drink too much). Address the reasons for the behavior, certainly, but understand that only the child himself can correct the behavior.

No one has a magic formula for raising well-behaved children, but through trial and error (sorry, child #1!), here are a few pointers which can help Supermom in some difficult times.

1) Never issue empty threats. Make sure the threat *can* be carried out, and *will* be carried out, then do it. Immediately. Avoid saying things like, "You will never be allowed cookies ever again," or "maybe I'll just cancel Christmas."

2) Make sure the amount of time allotted for a time-out is appropriate, as well as the timing. A three-year-old should be sent to their room for no longer than five minutes, immediately. An eleven-year-old can be sent to their room for a half hour, once dinner is over. Teenagers can be banished for semesters at a time if need be. Be sure to let kids know in advance it's okay to leave their room to go the bathroom.

3) Make sure the punishment fits the crime. Try not to act on your own anger at the time of the punishment. Banishing children from watching

television for a whole week simply because they have spilled some food in the family room is a bad idea. Those of you with children and TVs know who will *really* be punished during that week. (I've got to track my PMS schedule a little more closely.)

4) Let them clean up their own mess as punishment. Whether accidental or not, parents don't like a mess mostly because we have to clean it up. Make them do a load of laundry if they can't break the habit of using their shirt as a napkin or someone else's shirt as a Kleenex.

5) Recognize accidents do happen and try not to lecture too much, unless there are ways that they can avoid making the same mistake again. For example, throwing a water balloon down the stairs to their infant brother.

I know there are many more guidelines available in professional child rearing literature. Go to those to get more helpful hints if you feel you need them. Perhaps your *parenting coach* can help out. Just keep in mind the child's age, their temperament, their point of view, and their expectations. Try to do the most appropriate thing to ensure that they won't behave that way again.

Temper tantrums are probably the most frustrating childhood behavior. They are an attention-getter of the worst sort. Whatever you do, don't give in. Just let it go. Young children quickly learn that this can be an effective method for getting what they want, if you succumb to it. Speak in a quiet, forceful voice, and let them go to it. If you're in public, take them to the safety of a car or stroller seat. We've all been there. Tantrums do end eventually, especially if the child has learned that they are an ineffective way to communicate.

It sounds pretty basic, but know your children and what's important to them. Reward them as often as you punish them. If their bad behavior is solely for attention, make up a reward that gives them time alone with Mom or Dad. They'll learn that you want to spend time with them when they're acting in an appropriate manner. Acknowledge good behavior with compliments, so they can tell when you're pleased with them. As tempting as it may be, when they're really upset, try not to compare their behavior to other children's.

Watch your child for the times that she's stressed, and try not to impose other activities or demands on her at that time. It will increase the likelihood for misbehavior. Watch your *own* stressful times as well. If this is all day long, don't take it out on your child.

Children learn mostly by example. If the example they're seeing is *you* yelling and screaming when upset, or spanking them while espousing a "no hitting" rule, you're going to be in trouble. Life isn't a Mr. Rogers episode of sweetness and light, but put some effort into thinking about how to react yourself when things aren't going well in your "neighborhood." The best example of good behavior is your own.

PART 9:

The Quite
Serious
Advisory
Section of
the Book
(I'd Skip It)

"There is no reciprocity. Men love women, women love children, children love hamsters."

—Alice Thomas Ellis

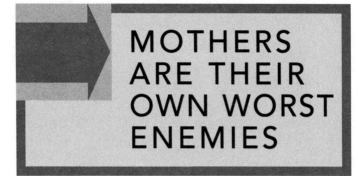

MOTHERS ARE THEIR OWN WORST ENEMIES

Supermoms are hard on themselves. They are also hard on others and the bar can be perpetually raised (see Ubermoms). Listen to the next conversation you are involved in with friends, and you'll see that most topics include the tearing down of either ourselves, or each other.

We do it to ourselves all the time. The most harmful way that we thwart our own efforts is the way in which women treat other women. The way many Supermoms disdain Homers. The way some Homers condemn Supermoms. Women who are too obsessed with their children versus those who don't care enough. It's not an easy job raising a family, whether both partners work or not. Why is it we run each other down in assessing and criticizing the techniques of others? Isn't there any room for compassion, apology, and understanding?

It's extremely hard to walk a mile in someone else's shoes, particularly when the owner of the shoes really annoys you, but it's important to try.

Oprah Winfrey often expounds on being spontaneously kind to strangers and friends and family alike. Random acts of kindness, she calls them. We need more of these. Not just holding open doors for a passing stroller, or helping to corral another's toddler, but real acts of kindness that go unnoticed. The next time you see a harried mother "losing it" with her young children in the supermarket, don't judge. Don't interfere or roll your eyes. Find it within yourself to feel some sympathy and understanding. You've only witnessed maybe five minutes of her entire day, and they could have well been her worst (or frighteningly enough, her best) five minutes of the month.

You often hear women who stay at home with their children complain their husbands never thank them for all the hard work they do around the house. They receive no recognition for the cleaning, cooking, driving, volunteering, bandaging, laundry, and all of the other mundane chores that make up their day. There are no "End of Year" awards or "Top Housewife" contests, and so they look to their spouse for some sort of praise and/or reward. Before these women challenge their husbands, they should ask themselves when the last time was that *they* thanked their husbands for allowing *them* the privilege and the pleasure of caring for their own children, in the comfort of their own home? Thanks for not only the money, which is mandatory, but also for the status, the pride, and the comfort that comes with a steady income, for all members of the family.

This is a two-way street and parents should encourage and support each other. You hear about the Mom who hands the baby over to the husband the minute he enters the front door, and announce that it is his turn to take over that duty, as she has done her share during the day. Question: if taking care of a baby during the day is as much work as going out to the office, then when does the father get his down time? This same woman doesn't pick up their husband's briefcase and carry on performing *his* work duties, so it doesn't seem to be a fair trade-off. It's nice to have someone to share the duty, no argument, but if I were the man receiving the baby, I would try to delay my arrival at home for as long as I could. That traveling sales position looks pretty good...

Homers do work physically hard for most of the day. Contrary to statements you might hear from skinny celebrity Ubermoms, this is still not enough to acquire and maintain a size zero body. One of the unique things about the Homer profession is the flexibility of the daily schedule. Even if one of these Moms is able to find half an hour to relax or do something for themselves during the day, it's a good half an hour more than her Supermom counterparts found, I can guarantee you. The Supermom has to schedule her pee breaks.

While the Homer, go-to-the-gym type of Mom does have many, many tedious tasks to perform, each day is slightly different than the one before, and much of their busy time is what others do for recreation. There may be a lack of recognition of the good things, and too much focus on the laundry that is done every day, the kid's lunches that are made every morning. Supermom does these chores as well. It's not fun doing the same hour-long commute every morning either. It might seem more glamorous and "fun" to work outside the home but the reality is that *fun* is often in short supply at the office. It would be interesting to see the results of a survey that measured the amount of smiling done by the Homer crowd versus the Supermom crowd. Or rather, the amount that should be done. Staying at home with your children can be a great gift.

We are very quick to judge those we think are

either vastly inferior or superior to us. Think about it the next time you find yourself condemning or disapproving of a certain type of behavior or situation. Why does the situation offend so much— would we have been able to handle it all that differently? Perhaps, but if not, remember each individual has different skills and talents. We can't all be brilliant at everything.

LET IT GO

We live in very stressful times. After all of mankind's efforts to create machines built for our convenience, to allow us more leisure time, we feel we have less time in the day than our ancestors did. We have washing machines to wash our clothes, but we wash them after each wear, instead of on a weekly or monthly basis as the pioneers did. We have dishwashers to wash our dishes, but we use approximately eighteen different receptacles to create a frozen dinner. We have answering machines to make us feel even guiltier about not returning calls. We have email that demands immediate attention versus paper, (or snail mail, which can be ignored for a good week, citing the inadequacies of the Post Office). Instant coffee, instant soup, frozen lasagnas, ready-cooked meals—all created to shave seconds or minutes off our time-pressured days. It begs the question—where has all of that accumulation of spare time gone?

While we have embraced these conveniences we have also created an illusion that things happen immediately and without human intervention. Anyone who does laundry on a regular basis knows that the sorting, folding, and putting away of even one load of laundry can take up to an hour or more with a large family. Putting things away in general takes a lot of time, from groceries to clean dishes. We all plan on emptying out our closets, desk drawers, kitchen drawers, and trunks and living somewhat minimal lives, but who has the time?

We have to let it go. Let go of the need to do everything. Babies do not *need* Halloween costumes. Children do not *need* home-baked brownies. Husbands do not *need* perfectly-ironed clothes. We do not *need* to look like supermodels all of the time (once a year would be nice, maybe). The house does not *need* to be spotless. Being a Supermom doesn't mean killing yourself to make things as perfect as they ultimately could be.

Play the game "worst possible conclusion." For example, what's the worst possible conclusion of not having the house spotless before friends arrive? They think you're messy. If they stop being your friends based on this one opinion, what kind of friends were they anyway? What's the worst possible conclusion of missing a bake sale at school? Someone notices. And that *someone* is probably someone who will then feel sanctimonious about always bringing in the baked goods. Let them have their day. You've just let it go.

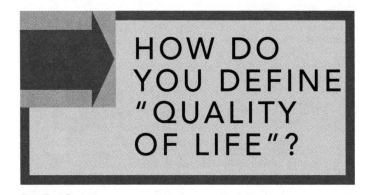

HOW DO YOU DEFINE "QUALITY OF LIFE"?

We've all met women like this: they return to work after their short maternity leave to a very challenging and professional role. They seem happy, busy, and exude a successful air. They take on the mantle of Supermom and they are doing it, goddammit. Yet, upon hearing the news that former colleague has decided to "opt out" of returning to the office, they are overheard to exclaim "Oh, the lucky dog. The quality of my life would improve immensely were I to stay at home with the children." This, from the mouth of a Supermom? Believe it.

Rampant Supermoms usually assume that quality of life has to be linked to money. Even Supermoms who could stay away from work for a while and still have a comfortable lifestyle. Nonetheless, healthy incomes are always sorely missed when it comes to vacation time, new clothing lines, and generally all the fun stuff. A decision to give up the second income is always significant.

What is sometimes incalculable is the time that you give up in your quest to perform all of the Supermom duties. Time that lets you watch your child paint, play in the snow, or take ten minutes deciding on a pair of unsuitable pants. As a Supermom, the trade-off is arriving home at 6:30 in the evening, after pining after them all day, only to wish it was their bedtime ten minutes later. It can be called "snapping." Your "snap" quota goes up considerably when the pressures of time and guilt pile up on you, and almost no amount of extra money can make up for that. Supermom has Superguilt. Guilt over leaving the office too soon and guilt over getting home too late. Guilt over missed homework, missed concerts, lost teeth, first steps, new foods, etc.

When the role of Supermom is relinquished for any sort of vacation, or leave, it can be nice knowing what your children's favorite snacks are, what television shows they like to watch after school, and which friends they are really close with. Just hearing about the interplay on the school bus is something you never thought you would be interested in, because you always have too many other things to do.

Many Supermoms have to work in order to contribute financially. For others it is a choice. Either way, they are faced with the additional stress and guilt and it can be extremely hard to relax during downtime with the children. Multitudes of undone tasks will race through Supermom's head as she nods vacantly to her children. It's hard to be in the here and now when your children are present. But that's the *real* quality time.

Instead of praying for an early bedtime for them, try to listen to the kids, talk to the kids, and just watch them grow and play, whenever you can find a minute. The laundry will always be there. The next time you hear the phrase "quality of life," think about what either makes your life a high-quality one today, or what it would take to get you there in the future. Most Supermoms are surprised to discover that more money isn't always the answer.

AND THE COMPETITION BEGINS... NOW!

Some couples complement each other, and some couples compete with each other. The latter certainly seems to be truer than the former. Supermoms love to compete—you don't get to be Super without trouncing someone Regular. Couples all over North America are arguing about who had the tougher day, who had the least amount of sleep, who changed the diaper last, who emptied the garbage, blah, blah, blah. Both sides seem to want to win in terms of being the loser. That's right. Supermoms *want* to have the toughest day, the hardest boss, the least sleep, the most aching back, the worst headache. I don't know why this is. I assume it's to prove that we work harder and suffer more to be a part of the family than our spouse does. Why this is something we want to prove, I'm not sure.

Supermoms and their husbands love to compete about intricate details of their work. Who had the most meetings, the most emails, the worst administrative assistant, the bitchiest boss? It's hard to put yourself into someone else's shoes, even if you live with them and can literally put yourself in their shoes at any time. "Men don't know how women feel" and "I can't understand women at all" are laments often heard by one sex about the other. Imagine this fantasy scenario: Your partner suddenly turns to you and said, "You're right. You win. You have it tougher than I do." Then what? What great prize is it that Supermom is looking to find? From that moment on every dirty diaper is theirs for the changing? Well, that would be a start. You might try to reverse things a bit in your house by a) sympathizing with your husband's moans and groans (no matter how lame), and b) recognize when you think he's had a tougher go of it than you have. It could make a difference in a Supermom house. He is also encouraged to say "You've had enough. Let me take over." (Stop giggling.)

This competitive phenomenon can show itself in discussions between friends. Again, whose baby gets the least amount of sleep, dirties the most diapers, screams the loudest, and makes the biggest messes. Then, sometime after the infant stage, it switches from the worst newborn to a contest for the "best" kid. The most advanced for his age (even if, at six months, it is the ability to hold a raisin in between two fingers), the tallest, the thinnest (this seems to matter even with babies), the most hair, the most teeth, sleeps the longest, eats the most, off the bottle first...It's exhausting, really. The strange thing about these contests is that most of the categories are things that the children themselves have no control over. You can't make a baby sit up before he's ready. They walk when they want to. They talk when they want to. They swear first when they want to. If the children don't have any control over when this happens, the parents have even less. Yet, we seem to think that we do. Supermoms have been known to even compare their college-aged children, the grades they get, the social life they have and the phrase "...but they were always like that" gets bandied about quite a bit. The competition goes on right through to the first grandchild, and eventually, I suppose, to the nicest funeral.

The next time you find yourself in one of these competitive arguments/discussions, try to see the other side and be objective. Try to take some of the pain away from the other person, instead of trying to find ways to magnify your own. Celebrate accomplishments and good days, rather than relishing failures and bad days. See the diaper as half empty, and life seems a little bit easier.

HOW TO LOOK LIKE A SUPERMOM

Most of the time, Supermoms feel they are not, in fact, Super and are failing in many key aspects of their lives. Take these practical tips to help turn things around.

1) Do not engage in fruitless worry. If worrying or thinking about a problem will not resolve it, don't waste the energy and lose the sleep. Don't sweat the small stuff. There are enough big things to worry about in the life of a Supermom.

2) Sacrifice quality for quantity. Supermom needs time to herself. Find time where you can. Get dinner on the table even if the table hasn't been wiped. Send your children to school in ripped jeans. Forget to check their homework once in a while. Get behind on the laundry. By sacrificing the "tidy up" issues in your life, you'll be able to free up five, ten, fifteen minutes or more a day to concentrate on the

most important thing—yourself. Read a magazine. Eat unshelled sunflower seeds without sticky fingers grabbing them. Go for a walk (not into a grocery store!). You'll appreciate it.

3) Do it now! Buy a gift for your sister's June birthday in November. Make dinner two hours early. Plan parties a month ahead of time. Register for courses as soon as the guide comes out. Buy loot bags when you see them on sale. Buy two or three pairs of shoes for your children at a time, in ever-increasing sizes, and store them until you need them. Buy bulk. The stress of last-minute details makes all situations worse than they need to be.

4) Don't whine, *do!* If you find yourself whining more than once about not having the time to do something, track the time it's taking you to complain, and use the time to *get it done*. If you have a two-hour lunch with friends and spend most of the time complaining about how you feel guilty that your four-year-old daughter's bedroom isn't decorated because you don't have the time, pick yourself up out of your well-warmed seat and march yourself into a paint store. Talk is cheap.

5) *Buy* time. There are several ways you can buy time, budget permitting. How many times have you left the dry cleaning drop off or pick up until the last possible second, often when it's too late?

There are many companies who will pick up dry cleaning from your front door and return it a few days later. The additional cost is typically minimal. Internet grocery shopping—in a word, nirvana. Many sad women will tell you that grocery shopping is "their time" and they don't want to give it up! Losers. The extra time *not* grocery shopping could be spent with your children, reading a book, having a glass of wine, walking on the beach, or shopping for shoes instead of milk.

There are cleaning women, gardening services, painters, etc., all ready to help, budget permitting. The stress of responsibility for these chores is almost as much effort as the chore itself—delegate these tasks as you would delegate tasks at work. It will be money well spent.

6) Let the phone ring. How many times has the phone rung in the middle of dinner? An important conversation? Your children's homework time? Let it ring—that's what answering machines and services are for. Return calls when it's convenient for *you*. Leave your email address on your message, if you prefer to communicate in that way. Don't let the person on the other end of the phone dictate how your time will be spent.

7) Keep a Saturday or Sunday for relaxing. Try to schedule only one social event each weekend, if

possible. The downtime is invaluable for de-stressing and getting things done.

8) Free yourself from little tasks. Ask yourself: is there one task that, if I don't get done today, will nag me again tomorrow? Cleaning out a closet, writing a thank-you card, ironing, returning a library book? These little tasks have a way of taking up inordinate amounts of think time when they're not checked off the list. Make it the first thing you do today, to get it out of your head.

Forget trying to achieve the ideal weight, the perfect house, and having your children always tidy and well-behaved. It ain't gonna happen, baby. Take pride in everything you do, and list your accomplishments mentally every day (or physically and post them on the fridge for you-know-who to read). Life is too short to be lived any other way.

AND THE WINNER IS...

If you entered into the world of the Supermom looking for admiration, praise, respect and a sense of accomplishment, whoa baby did you come to the wrong place. Most Supermoms are happy to make it to the end of the day with the following intact: their sanity, their house, their children, their job, their car, and their marriage. Anything else, like personal success, full kitchen cupboards, at least one clean bathroom, and a smile from their child and a passing neighbor is gravy.

Men don't understand it, women who don't work outside the home don't get it, and certainly the childless don't even come close to getting it. But that's okay. We've chosen this life, and we really wouldn't have it any other way. We are proud of the balance which we sometimes achieve in our lives, and we are willing to make the sacrifices required to get there. Except maybe the minivan.

We're proud of our unique life skills. For example, Supermoms have the uncanny ability to multitask in ways that Homers, Others, and Men cannot. Appearing to be professional and organized while giving a career-making presentation at work while simultaneously silently praying that your child's teacher will not notice the mysterious rash on Junior's arm for at least the next thirty minutes is a situation only Supermoms find themselves in. And yes, we're guilty about sending him in with the rash. And no, his father probably didn't notice, but yes, the Homer next door probably did as he was getting on to the school bus next to her perfect child.

We're not perfect, but we're certainly worthy of the title Super. Just remember ladies—we fought for this right, and we're going to make every attempt to make sure our daughters have the opportunity to work just as hard...aren't we?

BE SUPER

ABOUT THE AUTHOR

Kathy Buckworth was born in 1963 in Toronto, and raised in Winnipeg. She has a dormant degree in Political Science from York University as well as collecting various educational accoutrements at the University  of Alberta, the University of British Columbia, and Mount Royal College. She has gone through jobs like a baby goes through diapers: packaged goods marketing, freelance public relations, telecommunications product management, owning and operating a retail store, loyalty marketing, and her last position as a marketing director for a major Canadian bank. She is a frequent contributor to Toronto area publications, including *Toronto Families*, *Today's Parent*, *City Parent*, and the *Mississauga News*. She lives in Mississauga, Ontario, with her husband and four children. And. No. Dog. She is currently at work on her second book, *A Journey to the Darkside: Supermom Goes Home.* Visit her website at www.kathybuckworth.com